BASIC TEACHINGS OF THE BIBLE
Questions Christians Ask—Biblical Answers
VOLUME 2

Edward D. Andrews

BASIC TEACHINGS OF THE BIBLE

Questions Christians Ask—Biblical Answers

VOLUME 2

Edward D. Andrews

ISBN-13: **978-0692023754**

ISBN-10: **0692023755**

Christian Publishing House
Cambridge, Ohio
BASIC TEACHINGS OF THE BIBLE Questions Christians Ask—Biblical Answers VOLUME 2
Copyright © 2014 by Christian Publishing House

support@christianpublishers.org

All rights reserved. Except for brief quotations in articles, other publications, book reviews, and blogs, no part of this book may be reproduced in any manner without prior written permission from the publishers.

Edward D. Andrews is to be identified as the author of this work.

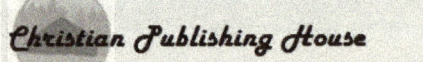

INTRODUCTION 7

BASIC TEACHING: Why Study the Bible? . 9

    Imitation Christians Are Sifted Out.......22

    Recommended Publications..................26

BASIC TEACHING: Where Did God Come From?... 28

    The Use of Logic 28

    What About the Beginning 31

    Something Cannot Come From Nothing 33

    Life Comes From Life 35

    Our Universe Has a Purpose................37

BASIC TEACHING: Is Speaking in Tongues Evidence of True Christianity?................. 39

    Modern-day Speaking in Tongues........43

    What is the Real Force Behind Today's Speaking in Tongues? 48

    As for Tongues, They Will Cease..........56

    Final Thoughts 60

BASIC TEACHING: Do We Have a Soul that Is Apart From Us? 62

    A Soul Breathes...................................62

Soul as "a living creature" 64

Soul as the Life of the Creature 70

Can the Soul Die? 75

Soul Departing and Soul Coming into a Person... 80

Excursion Literal versus Dynamic Equivalent 82

His Spirit Goes Forth and He Returns to the Earth 86

BASIC TEACHING: Does Abortion Show Respect for Life? 91

The Human Fetus 92

Are Unborn Children Worth Less in the Eyes of God? 93

What is the Punishment for Taking a Human Life? 102

Early Christians on Abortion 102

The Teaching of the Bible 103

Scarred Emotionally for Life 104

Get the Help and Care 106

BASIC TEACHING: Does the Bible Teach Universal Salvation? 107

The Salvation Debate 109

The Bible Teaches 111

Unbiblical Teaching........................... 121

BASIC TEACHING: What Is Inerrancy of Scripture?... 125

The Foundational Doctrine................ 136

BASIC TEACHING: Does the Bible Teach Liberation Theology?............................ 140

Liberation Theology and the Pope..... 144

The Church Set Against the Theologians 146

Liberation Theology Set Against the Bible 146

True Liberation 150

An Erroneous Philosophy 159

How Can We Really Help the Poor? . 162

BASIC TEACHING: Does It Matter Which Bible Translation?................................... 166

The Bible Translation Debate............. 166

BASIC TEACHING: Was Job a Real Historical Person? 173

Other Books Authored by Edward D. Andrews 183

BASIC TEACHINGS OF THE BIBLE Questions Christians Ask—Biblical Answers 183

WALK HUMBLY WITH YOUR GOD: Putting God's Purpose First in Your Life ...186

APPLYING GOD'S WORD MORE FULLY IN YOUR LIFE: How to Broaden and Deepen Your Understanding of God's Word 188

MISREPRESENTING JESUS: Debunking Bart D. Ehrman's Misquoting Jesus.............190

THE TEXT OF THE NEW TESTAMENT: A Beginner's Guide to New Testament Textual Criticism..192

THE COMPLETE GUIDE TO BIBLE TRANSLATION: Bible Translation Choices and Translation Principles 194

YOUR GUIDE FOR DEFENDING THE BIBLE: Self-Education of the Bible Made Easy 196

AN INTRODUCTION TO BIBLE DIFFICULTIES: So-called Errors and Contradictions... 200

INTRODUCTION

Basic Teachings of the Bible is a **series** of books that cover the Questions Christians ask, with biblical answers,

- Why Study the Bible?
- Where Did God Come From?
- Is Speaking in Tongues Evidence of True Christianity?
- Do We Have a Soul that Is Apart From Us?
- Does Abortion Show Respect for Life?
- Do We Possess a Soul or Are We a Soul?
- Does the Bible Teach Universal Salvation?
- What Is Inerrancy of Scripture?
- Does the Bible Teach Liberation Theology?
- Does It Matter Which Bible Translation?
- Was Job a Real Historical Person?

These are the type of basic Bible questions that are discussed and debated, before and after church services, at Christian gatherings, and on the internet. There are literally hundreds of them. These are questions that Bible critics might raise as well, which Christians have struggled to answer and now will have a simplified biblical response. The Bible will give us the answers to these questions, as well as reasoning and explaining from the Scriptures. If the texts are straightforward, which answer the question(s), the text alone will be used. However, if the text is difficult to understand, reasoning from the Scriptures will be used with the text. We will answer some of the questions in just 2-3 pages, while some may take up to 15 pages or more. It is hoped that the reader will find the answers as additional evidence demonstrating that the Bible is the best source for guiding one's life. This publication is **VOLUME 2** of numerous volumes to come.

BASIC TEACHING: Why Study the Bible?

When Christians talk among themselves about the Bible, we generally hear, "I believe," "I think," "As I understand it," "I feel," "The way I see it is," and so on. For example, John says, when Jesus said, 'whoever divorces his wife, except on the basis of sexual immorality, and marries another commits adultery,' I believe Jesus did not mean there was an exception." Then, James responds, "Well, that's your belief, but I see it as an exception." Jesus would never suggest that it would be fine if another saw it different from him, as though there could be two different meanings of a text, and both could be right. In looking at Jesus' conversations, where he quote Scripture over 120 times, there was either one correct understanding, one correct meaning to a text, and your understanding of it was either right or wrong, true or false, there was no middle ground, no gray, open-ended, in-between position, when it came to truth and error.

When it comes to Jesus and the New Testament writer's interpretation of text that they quoted or referred to, they were right, true, accurate, as Holy Spirit moved them to pen what they wrote. They had absolutely no doubt in the things they taught, as they spoke with certainty. The New Testament writers never viewed Hebrew Scriptures or Jesus' words as some guitar, which can be picked up and tuned to anyone's liking. Rather, they saw Jesus' Words, and the Old Testament, as the Word of God, that had but one meaning, i.e., what the author meant by his words, not what Jimmy, Frank, Bobby, Julie or anyone else thinks, feels, or believes it means; unless, they have hit upon the actual, true one meaning.

You will take note that Jesus was the Son of God, yet he always based everything he said on the Word of God as his authority. Of course, it is true that the Father gave him all authority, but even so, you never hear him offering his opinion; instead, he referred to Scripture. This is an example, which we do well to follow. The Bible was inspired of God, and Jesus came to earth as a representative of the Father, who selected the eight authors to pen the twenty-seven Greek New Testament books that would be added to the thirty-nine Hebrew Scripture books.

Remember when Satan was tempting Jesus? In his temptations, Satan quoted Scripture, in his effort to tempt Jesus to sin against the Father. Satan said to Jesus, "If you are the Son of God, throw yourself down, for it is written, "'He will command his angels concerning you,' and "'on their hands they will bear you up, lest you strike your foot against a stone.'" Jesus did not respond, "That is *your* understanding." On all three temptations, responded to Satan as such, "It is written," and then quoted Scripture as his authority. The quotation of Psalm 91:11-12 by Satan was misused and misapplied. Notice below, the pattern of Jesus' pattern proving things to others,

Matthew 4:4 English Standard Version (ESV)

⁴ But he answered, "**It is written,**

"'Man shall not live by bread alone,
but by every word that comes from the
mouth of God.'" **[Deuteronomy 8:3]**

Matthew 4:7 English Standard Version (ESV)

⁷ Jesus said to him, "**Again it is written,** 'You shall not put the Lord your God to the test.'" **[Deuteronomy 6:16]**

Matthew 4:10 English Standard Version (ESV)

¹⁰ Then Jesus said to him, "Be gone, Satan! For **it is written,**

"'You shall worship the Lord your God and him only shall you serve.'"
[Deuteronomy 10:20]

Matthew 11:10 English Standard Version (ESV)

¹⁰ This is he of whom **it is written**,

"'Behold, I send my messenger before your face,
who will prepare your way before you.'
[Malachi 3:1; Isaiah 40:3]

Matthew 21:13 English Standard Version (ESV)

¹³ He said to them, "**It is written**, 'My house shall be called a house of prayer,' but you make it a den of robbers." **[Jeremiah 7:11]**

Matthew 26:24 English Standard Version (ESV)

²⁴ The Son of Man goes as **it is written** of him, but woe to that man by whom the Son of Man is betrayed! It would have been better for that man if he had not been born." **[Deuteronomy 27:25]**

Matthew 26:31 English Standard Version (ESV)

³¹ Then Jesus said to them, "You will all fall away because of me this night. For **it is written**, 'I will strike the shepherd, and the sheep of the flock will be scattered.' **[Zechariah 13:7]**

Jesus had condemned the self-righteous Pharisees on numerous occasions, using the words of Isaiah. Jesus said to them, "Well did Isaiah prophesy of you hypocrites, as it is written, "'this people honors me with their lips, but their heart is far from me.'" (Mark 7:6) Once while in the Synagogue in Nazareth, he read from the book Isaiah, demonstrating his commission from God that he was to preach the Word, "The Spirit of the Lord is upon me, because he has anointed me to proclaim good news to the poor. He has sent me to proclaim liberty to the captives and recovering of sight to the blind, to set at liberty those who are oppressed, to proclaim the year of the Lord's favor." (Lu 4:18-19) When questioned about everlasting life, Jesus said, "What is written in the Law? How do you read it?" The one questioning him responded, "You shall love the Lord your God with all your heart and with all your soul and with all your strength and with all your mind, and your neighbor as yourself." And he said to him, "You have answered correctly; do this, and you will live."

(Lu 10:25-28) On another occasion, Jesus explains from the Hebrew Scriptures that it was written; he would be rejected and killed. And taking the twelve, Jesus said to them, "See, we are going up to Jerusalem, and everything that is written about the Son of Man by the prophets will be accomplished. For he will be delivered over to the Gentiles and will be mocked and shamefully treated and spit upon. And after flogging him, they will kill him, and on the third day he will rise." (Lu 18:31-33) Jesus even shared the prophecies about his resurrection as well. Then he said to them, "These are my words that I spoke to you while I was still with you, that everything written about me in the Law of Moses and the Prophets and the Psalms must be fulfilled." Then he opened their minds to understand the Scriptures, and said to them, "Thus it is written, that the Christ should suffer and on the third day rise from the dead" (Lu 24:44-46)

Clearly, Jesus had an outstanding knowledge of the Hebrew Scriptures. Moreover, Jesus had an accurate understanding of the Hebrew Scriptures. The same Scriptures that the Jewish religious leaders twisted with their oral traditions, to oppress and abuse the common people, Jesus used correctly to raise them up, and offer them hope. Jesus condemned the Jewish religious leaders, saying they had made 'void the word of God by their tradition that they had handed down.' (Mark 7:13) We should never read our personal opinions into the text, but rather ascertain what the author meant by his words to his audience; then, see if there are any implications for us.

Jesus' first century disciples knew the Hebrew Scriptures quite well.[1] There are 320 direct quotations from the Hebrew Scriptures. According to a listing published by Westcott and Hort, the combined total of quotations and references is some 890. Jesus' disciples saw the Old Testament as the inspired, inerrant Word of God, which guided them in life. For example, Paul wrote, "I worship the God of our fathers, believing everything laid down by the Law and written in the Prophets." (Ac 24:14) Luke referenced Isaiah, when he wrote, "As it is written in the book of the words of Isaiah the prophet, "The voice of one crying in the wilderness: 'Prepare the way of the Lord, make his paths straight.'" (Luke 3:4/Isa 40:3) The apostle John wrote, "His disciples

---

[1] As Matthew was writing to a Hebrew audiences, he quoted from the Hebrew Old Testament, while other New Testament writers quote or referenced the *Septuagint* Greek version of the Old Translation.

remembered that it was written, 'Zeal for your house will consume me.'" (John 2:17/Ps 69:9) John also wrote, "And Jesus found a young donkey and sat on it, just as it is written, 'Fear not, daughter of Zion; behold, your king is coming, sitting on a donkey's colt!'" (John 12:14-15/Zech. 9:9) Luke wrote in the book of Acts, "this he has fulfilled to us their children by raising Jesus, as also it is written in the second Psalm, 'You are my Son, today I have begotten you.'" (Ac 13:33) True enough, the early Christians knew the Old Testament well, and followed the counsel of Proverbs,

Proverbs 3:5-6 American Standard Version (ASV)

⁵ Trust in Jehovah with all your heart, And do not lean on your own understanding:

⁶ In all your ways acknowledge him, And he will direct your paths.

Every Bible verse has but one meaning, what the author intended by the words that he used. Therefore, why is it critical that we ascertain the correct meaning, the right knowledge? This is answered by Jesus himself, when he wrote, ""Not everyone who says to me, 'Lord, Lord,' will enter the kingdom of heaven, but **the one who does the will of my Father** who is in heaven." (Matt 7:21)

Who will benefit from the kingdom? 'The one doing the will of the Father.' How do we know the will of the Father? We know his will by having an accurate understanding of his Word, the Bible. Otherwise, Jesus went on to say, "On that day many will say to me, 'Lord, Lord, did we not prophesy in your name, and cast out demons in your name, and do many mighty works in your name?' And then will I declare to them, 'I never knew you; depart from me, you workers of lawlessness.'" (Matt 7:22-23) The apostle John wrote, "The world [of wicked humankind] is passing away along with its desires, but whoever does the will of God abides forever." Who abides forever? The one who abides forever is the one doing the will of God. How do we know the will of God?

Proverbs 2:1-6 American Standard Version (ASV)

¹ My son, if **you** will receive my words
   and treasure up my commandments with **you**,
² so as to incline **your** ear to wisdom
   and apply **your** heart to understanding;
³ Yes, if **you** cry after discernment
   and lift up **your** voice for understanding,
⁴ if **you** seek it as silver
   and search for it as for hidden treasures,
⁵ then **you** will understand the fear of Jehovah

and find the knowledge of God.
⁶ For Jehovah gives wisdom;
from his mouth come knowledge and understanding;

However, once you understand the "knowledge of God," you must then apply that knowledge in a correct and balanced manner. Paul said Jesus "became the source of eternal salvation to all who obey him." However, take note those words: "to all who obey him." How can you obey, if you do not have a correct understanding of Scripture? What did Paul say of young Timothy? He said, "From childhood you have been acquainted with the sacred writings, which are able to make you wise for salvation through faith in Christ Jesus." (2 Tim 3:15)

The faith that Timothy possessed was grounded in truths, reason, understanding and trust. It is based on "the knowledge of God." Timothy came to know and understand why Jesus had to offer himself as a ransom, and what it resulted in, as all of humanity now has an opportunity at eternal life. Knowledge of God's Word applied, results in faith in the things heard. The Bible is the Book that will build this faith, as it is "living and active, sharper than any two-edged sword, piercing to the division of soul and of spirit, of joints and of marrow, and discerning the thoughts and intentions of the heart." (Heb. 4:12)

Now, here comes the question that has some confused. If the Bible is so powerful, why are there 41,000 different Christian denominations? Why is there so much division? Why are so many Christians suffering spiritual shipwreck? It is because of biblical illiteracy. Over 90 percent of Christianity is biblically illiterate. Many pastors do not know how to turn this around, because they are actually the ones dumbing the members of the church down. What I am about to say will hurt the feelings of some, and anger others, but it must be said.

Christians, true Christians love Christ and will do what is expected of them. We are not looking for imitation Christians and the churches are full of them, ones looking for a social club to be a part of, but are not committed to obeying the Word of God to the fullest extent possible. There is no real Bible education in the churches, as most Bible study classes are studying out of a feel good booklet, written on a sixth grade level. The church members are not educated in the Bible, about the Bible, nor the doctrine of the faith. They are not trained evangelist, because most churches believe that its members are not intelligent enough, nor will they buy out the time.

However, the truth is, the Christians that we are looking for, are those who will, like Jesus and the apostles, and other first century Christians, will take in knowledge of God's Word, as well as buy out time to understand its true meaning. Then, they will apply that Word as they are taught to be evangelists in their own communities, taking the great commission as serious as the pastor does. (Matt 28:19-20) They will transform their lives as they correctly apply God's Word. Yes, they are 'transformed by the renewal of their mind, that by testing they may discern what is the will of God, what is good and acceptable and perfect.' (Rom 12:2) These ones faith would grow strong, their course would be wise, and if they actual had the knowledge of God, and acted on it properly, as they would be 'doing the will of God and abiding forever.' (1 John 2:17) Such faith and knowledge is being withheld from these true Christians, as pastors have low expectations, because, they are so busy trying to please the world, and imitation Christians, that they are keeping the core flock as spiritual babes.

Hebrews 5:11-6:1 English Standard Version (ESV)

11 About this we have much to say, and it is hard to explain, since you have become dull of hearing. **12** For though by this time you ought to be teachers, you need someone to teach you again the basic principles of the oracles of God. You need milk, not solid food, **13** for everyone who lives on milk is unskilled in the word of righteousness, since he is a child. **14** But solid food is for the mature, for those who have their powers of discernment trained by constant practice to distinguish good from evil.

6 Therefore let us leave the elementary doctrine of Christ and go on to maturity, not laying again a foundation of repentance from dead works and of faith toward God

True faith and knowledge comes from God's Word. We simply need our pastors to preach and teach, raising the bar of expectations, so the true Christians can remain, while the imitation Christians can be sifted out. True, some Christians will be sifted out because they will not loyally submit to God's Word, nor God's pastor (Heb. 13:17), if the bar of expectation is raised. However, many true Christians will prove obedient to God's Word and be submissive to the pastor taking the lead in the congregation.

Imitation Christians Are Sifted Out

Harvesting in the days of Jesus took much effort and time, and was generally a family affair. Looking at the wheat harvest, it takes place in four stages; **(1)** the one **harvesting** would gather the wheat stalks from the field. **(2)** Then, they would beat these stalks against a hard surface, or use an animal to pull the **threshing** sled. This procedure would free the grain from the stalks and the husks. **(3)** Then there is the **winnowing** process, where the workers would toss the mixture into the air, to separate grain from its husks. The kernels would fall back onto the threshing floor, whereas the wind would blow the seed coverings away. **(4)** Lastly, the kernels were cautiously **sifted** to remove from them any unwanted, unwelcomed, objectionable materials. "Jesus spoke often of the harvest in connection with the harvesting of souls (Matt. 9:37; Mark 4:29; John 4:35). In the parable of the tares, Jesus related harvest to the end of the world (Matt. 13:30–39). The rhythm of harvest time (sowing and reaping) provided an illustration of a spiritual truth (Gal. 6:7–8)."[2] If a church would truly teach and train their flock, with high expectations, those who are not rightly

---

[2] http://biblia.com/books/hlmnillbbldict/Page.p_721

disposed toward life, because they do not have a receptive heart, will be sifted out. It all hinges on the evangelism work.

Because almost no churches have an evangelism program, almost no Christians are aware of the extraordinary joy associated with 'making disciples by teaching them.' Paul and his more than one hundred traveling companions knew this special joy all too well.

1 Thessalonians 2:19-20

English Standard Version (ESV)

¹⁹ For what is our hope or joy or crown of boasting before our Lord Jesus at his coming? Is it not you? ²⁰ For you are our glory and joy.

2:19. Here Paul gives a glimpse into why he was so persistent. These people were his **hope, joy,** and **crown**. Paul understood life today in the light of the eternity to come. He built the present upon the certainty of the future. Everything pointed toward that day when he would stand in the presence of Christ. He knew that people were the treasure and glory for which God worked and suffered. Paul's vision of life centered upon people because he knew that all of God's revelation—from creation through the prophets to Christ himself—was intended to redeem people.

2:20. To Paul, the Thessalonian believers were **our glory and joy**. God is interested in people. The heavens are his, the mountains are the work of his hand, the oceans are his handiwork—but people are his pride and treasure. Like Paul, we should express our love to others, treasuring the moments when people come to faith in Christ.[3]

Paul was very aware of the joy that came with making disciples, which he wrote about in his letter to the Thessalonians. He knew the joy of watching the happiness of newly interested ones as they came to know biblical truth, the life changing effects as they applied those truths in their lives. We too can share in that joy, the joy of having spiritual children that we have brought to Christ.

The most effect way of making disciples is by finding one who will listen and eventually

---

[3] Knute Larson, *I & II Thessalonians, I & II Timothy, Titus, Philemon*, vol. 9, Holman New Testament Commentary (Nashville, TN: Broadman & Holman Publishers, 2000), 28.

accept the truths that you share in conversation. You may find this one by informally witnessing to someone, or in the phone ministry of the church, or street witnessing, or in the house-to-house ministry, or within your family or friends, coworkers, and so on.

Once you have been sharing the truths with this one for a time, you need to invite them to the Christian services, and this may mean your offering them a ride if they need one. After they have attended a few meetings, they need a structured Bible study between you, the teacher, and this newly interested one. There are three different books, which you will need to study with your Bible student:

(1) Basic Bible Interpretation

(2) Basic Bible doctrines

(3) Spiritual and Personal Growth

Here are several books recommended for (1), (2) and (3). They are listed with the first being the one we would prefer. Of the two on biblical interpretation, *Basic Bible Interpretation* by Zuck is a little more difficult, and it does not have end of chapter questions. You would have to produce them before using his book. *A Basic Guide to Interpreting the Bible* is easier to understand, and has end of chapter questions.

Of the three on Bible doctrines, *Concise Bible Doctrines* by Towns is the easiest to understand. However, *Bible Doctrine: Essential Teachings of the Christian Faith* by Wayne Grudem has review questions, as well as questions for reflection at the end of each chapter. Of the two on Spiritual and Personal Growth, *Walk Humbly with Your God* by Edward D. Andrews is the preferred choice. It has review questions at the end of each chapter. However, you may want to offer *Read the Bible for Life* by George Guthrie, as a recommended reading. Below are the books.

Recommended Publications

Basic Bible Interpretation

(1) **Basic Bible Interpretation** by Roy B. Zuck (Jan 1991)

(2) **A Basic Guide to Interpreting the Bible, Playing by the Rules** by Robert H. Stein (Jun 1, 2011)

Basic Bible Doctrines

(1) **Bible Doctrine: Essential Teachings of the Christian Faith** by Wayne Grudem and Jeff Purswell (Jul 12, 1999)

(2) **Introducing Christian Doctrine(2nd Edition)** by Erickson, Millard J. and Hustad, L. (Apr 1, 2001)

(3) **AMG Concise Bible Doctrines (AMG Concise Series)** by Towns, Elmer (Oct 30, 2011)

Spiritual Growth

(1) **Walk Humbly With Your God: Putting God's Purpose First in Your Life** by Andrews, Edward D. and Prince, Bruce (Apr 29, 2013)

(2) **Read the Bible for Life: Your Guide to Understanding and Living God's Word** by Guthrie, George (Dec 2, 2013)

(3) **Read the Bible for Life (Workbook)** by George H. Guthrie (Jan 3, 2011)

BASIC TEACHING: Where Did God Come From?

The common question thrown at Christians by the skeptics, agnostics and atheists is, "Where did God come from?" "Who or what created God?" They feel that this is the one obstacle, which cannot be overcome. It was the French philosopher Voltaire,[4] who said, "Si Dieu n'existait pas, il faudrait l'inventer," (If God did not exist, it would be necessary to invent him.)[5] Simply put, If God did not exist; we would have to invent him. Voltaire believed in God, but if someone proved God did not exist, people would have to invent God.

If we were asked the above questions, how would we respond? Here is how you might develop you argumentation.

The Use of Logic

The human mind struggles to comprehend the notion of something or someone having no beginning, which will also never end. To the

---

[4] **François-Marie Arouet** (also known as **Voltaire**) was a French philosopher. He was born in 1694 and died in 1778.

[5] http://www.lpboulder.org/quotes

human mind, the view of time is linear. However, many now know that the universe had a cause of some sort, as it had a beginning. When we think of that cause, it is **illogical <u>not</u>** to view that cause with certain powers and qualities, such as energy, organizing ability, artistic taste, love, and wisdom. Why? Take some time, and ponder the thinks that you see around you every day. Think of just how organized our universe is, especially the intricacy of our solar system, and how life could not exist, if anything were of by the smallest of measures.

Our earth is the exact distance from the sun; otherwise, life would never exist. Astronomer John Barrow and mathematician Frank Tipler studied "the ratio of the Earth's radius and distance from the Sun." The final analysis from their study was that human life could never exist if "this ratio [was] slightly different from what it is observed to be." Professor David L. Block stated, "Calculations show that had the earth been situated only 5 per cent closer to the sun, a runaway greenhouse effect [causing the earth to overheat] would have occurred about 4 000 million years ago. If, on the other hand, the earth were placed only 1 per cent further from the sun, runaway glaciation [enormous sheets of ice would cover most of the earth] would have occurred some 2 000 million years ago."[6]

Christian philosopher Alvin Plantinga argues,

> One reaction to these apparent enormous coincidences is to see them as substantiating the theistic claim that the Universe has been created by a personal God and as offering the material for a properly restrained theistic argument—hence the fine-tuning argument. It's as if there are a large number of dials that have to be tuned to within extremely narrow limits for life to be possible in our Universe. It is extremely unlikely that this should happen by chance, but much more likely that this should happen, if there is such a person as God.[7]

---

[6] David L. Bock, *Our Universe: Accident or Design?* (1993)
[7] Alvin Plantinga, "The Dawkins Confusion; Naturalism ad absurdum," *Christianity Today*, March/April 2007
http://www.philvaz.com/apologetics/DawkinsGodDelusionPlantingaReview.pdf

Again, it would be illogical to look at the fine-tuning of our universe, especially our solar system, and not see design, requiring a designer, who possesses the characteristics mentioned above. It should be noted that the above attributes could not belong to a thin, but only to a person. Therefore, our designer is the all-powerful, loving Creator, God of the Bible.

What About the Beginning

When we look around our earth, our solar system, our galaxy, or our universe, we see a material universe. Within our planet earth, we see many different life forms. This brings us to the age-old question of, "where do we come from?" Science has long argued that life came about by chance. Of course, scientist and their theories generally presuppose the existence of something, regardless of what name they give it. Science rightly states that matter is a form of energy. Base on this, it is their educated guess that the material universe came about by accident more than 20 billion years ago. However, the sticking point for them is our question to them, "how did the material universe come about?" For the atheist scientists, they always have some preexistent *something* the beginning of which they are unable to explain.

Therefore, you have the atheists presupposing a *thing*. One the other hand, Christians presuppose the existence of a personal Creator, God. However, when we logically contemplate the natural laws, mathematical meticulousness, fine-tuning, organization, and wisdom apparent on earth and throughout our universe, what must we conclude? For Christians, we logically see the cause of our material universe as a Person not a thing, an intelligent, all-powerful Creator as opposed to some accident or chance, some blind force. Christians say, "In the beginning, God created the heavens and the earth" (Genesis 1:1), while atheist say, "In the beginning, *something* created the heavens and the earth." (Atheism 101)

For the atheist, liberal-progressive mindset, any documents found in antiquity are considered historical evidence, with the exception of Bible manuscripts. There are tens of thousands of Bible manuscripts, some dating to 200-300 B.C.E. Therefore, atheists do not like Christians quoting Bible manuscripts from antiquity, but it would be fine if you quote any other ancient document. However, the Bible's point of view is logical and consistent with apparent truths. Let us take a moment to examine a few.

Something Cannot Come From Nothing

French Philosopher and mathematician Descartes' causal argument is expressed as follows, "there must be at least as much reality in the efficient and total cause as in the effect of that cause," which in turn suggests that something cannot come from nothing. (AT VII 40: CSM II 28) What Descartes is saying is a causal theory that suggests, "Whatever is possessed by an effect must have been given to it by its cause. For example, when a pot of water is heated to a boil, it must have received that heat from some cause that had at least that much heat. Moreover, something that is not hot enough cannot cause water to boil, because it does not have the requisite reality to bring about that effect. In other words, something cannot give what it does not have."[8]

Science has never been able to prove that something can come from nothing. Human personal experience is that we are only able to create and build upon materials that already exist. It would be simply silly to suggest the material universe came out of nothing, because nothing is just that, nothingness. The Bible states the actual truth of the matter, "For every house

---

[8] http://www.iep.utm.edu/descarte/#SH5a

is built by someone, but the builder of all things is God." (Hebrew 3:4) We all, , even atheists, like the Bible, recognize that a house needs both an architect and a builder, but atheists then move on to suggest a far more complex atom, molecule, or cell came from nothingness, which simply defies reasonableness. Note the logicalness of the Bible,

Isaiah 29:16 English Standard Version (ESV)

[16] You turn things upside down!
Shall the potter be regarded as the clay,
that the thing made should say of its maker,
   "He did not make me";
or the thing formed say of him who formed it,
   "He has no understanding"?

Apologist William Lane Craig says,

> Believe it or not there are some atheists who actually think nothing can do something. Aside from the fact that this is obviously a self-contradiction (what's next, saying square-circles exist?!), now they think quantum physics (via virtual particles) is an example of something coming from nothing! William Lane Craig explains that the quantum vacuum is not nothing, because it's something -

namely, fluctuating energy. Unfortunately, atheists have resorted to pseudo-science when it comes to refuting the Kalam Cosmological Argument.[9]

Life Comes From Life

Even as science moves toward a designer (i.e., Creator), as each year passes, some still carry on in their belief that life came suddenly from nonliving matter. If life came about spontaneously, why is it that man, in this scientific era has yet to repeat and develop the process. Simply put, because we know that all known that living things come from other living things. Again, it is the Bible, which gives humanity true logic,

Psalm 90:2 English Standard Version (ESV)

[2] Before the mountains were brought forth,
    or ever you had formed the earth and the world,
    from everlasting to everlasting you are God.

Psalm 93:2 English Standard Version (ESV)

[2] Your throne is established from of old;
    you are from everlasting.

---

[9] http://www.youtube.com/watch?v=-BTT62YJCl8

Psalm 36:9 English Standard Version (ESV)

⁹ For with you is the fountain of life;
in your light do we see light.

Is Matter a Form of Energy?

Science has rightly stated that matter is a form of energy, but the Bible has supported this long ago. It was only in the last century that modern man has come to the realization of how to release energy from matter in atom bombs and in nuclear power stations. However, the Bible 2,700 years ago directed us to the source of energy that is locked up in our material universe.

Isaiah 40:26 English Standard Version (ESV)

²⁶ Lift up your eyes on high and see [the universe]:
who created these?
He who brings out their host by number,
calling them all by name,
by the greatness of his might,
and because he is strong in power
not one is missing.

Jeremiah 10:12 English Standard Version (ESV)

¹² It is he who made the earth by his power,
who established the world by his wisdom,

and by his understanding stretched out the heavens.

Our Universe Has a Purpose

When we think of the design, the order of the universe, its fine-tuning, we know that there has to have been a purpose for its existence. Does order ever result from disorder and confusion? Think of the earth's seasons and cycles, and their support of plant, animal, and human life. Does this sound as though it came about by chance? Reasonably, they give evidence of design and a designer, who had a purpose for our earth, our solar system, our galaxy and the other 125 billion galaxies in our universe of billions of universes. Think about it just for a minute, what a never-ending backyard humanity has. Our natural desire is to see what lies beyond the next hillside. Imagine, the billions of universes, which are continuously growing, giving us an eternity of exploration. What was the purpose of an all-wise, an all-powerful, all-knowing, all-loving Creator?

Isaiah 45:18 Updated American Standard Version (UASV)

[18] For thus says Jehovah,
who created the heavens
 he is God!,

who formed the earth and made it
 he established it;
he did not create it empty,
 he formed it to be inhabited!:
"I am Jehovah, and there is no other.

Psalm 115:16 American Standard Version (ASV)

[16] The heavens are the heavens of Jehovah,
 but the earth he has given to the sons of man.

BASIC TEACHING: Is Speaking in Tongues Evidence of True Christianity?

An extraordinary gift conveyed through the Holy Spirit to a number of disciples starting at Pentecost 33 C.E. that made it possible for them to speak or otherwise glorify God in a tongue in addition to their own.

What Was the Reason for the Speaking in Tongues?

Immediately before his ascension to heaven, Jesus told those who were looking on: "you will receive power when the Holy Spirit has come upon you, and you will be my witnesses in Jerusalem and in all Judea and Samaria, and to the end of the earth." (Acts 1:8, ESV) First, this witnessing campaign was to be of epic proportions; and second, it was to be brought about with the help of the Holy Spirit.

Our modern-day world allows the spread of the gospel to the other side of the globe within a millisecond and in any language. In the first-century, the good news was spread either in written form, orally, or both. Therefore, the ability to be miraculously able to speak a foreign language in the melting pot of that Roman Empire would have been greatly appreciated. This miracle was first realized at the Pentecost 33 C.E. celebration, as the first-century Christians began to witness to the Jews and proselytes in Jerusalem.

Acts 2:5-11, 41 English Standard Version (ESV)

⁵ Now there were dwelling in Jerusalem Jews, devout men from every nation under heaven. ⁶ And at this sound the multitude came together, and they were bewildered, because each one was hearing them speak in his own language. ⁷ And they were amazed and astonished, saying, "Are not all these who are speaking Galileans? ⁸ And how is it that we hear, each of us in his own native language? ⁹ Parthians and Medes and Elamites and residents of Mesopotamia, Judea and Cappadocia, Pontus and Asia, ¹⁰ Phrygia and Pamphylia, Egypt and the parts of Libya belonging to Cyrene, and visitors from Rome, ¹¹ both Jews and proselytes, Cretans and Arabians—we hear them telling in our own tongues the mighty works of God." ⁴¹ So those who received his word were baptized, and there were added that day about three thousand souls.

A major change was in the offing. The Jews had followed the lead of their religious leaders in the last act of rebellion, resulting in their rejection as his people. The Mosaic Law was being replaced with the law of Christ. This does not mean that no Jew could be received into the newly founded Christian congregation. To the contrary, the next three and half years would be only the Jewish people, who would make up this new way to God. As was the case with Moses, there was to be a sign, miraculous events, which included the speaking in tongues, this as evidence to those, whose heart was receptive to the truth that the Son of God had come, had given his life for them, and ascended back to heaven. Exodus 19:16-19

Speaking in tongues in Acts 2 is evidentiary. The unique speech is demonstrable proof that something supernatural has happened to the 120 disciples of Jesus. Tongues are the sign that these people have received the promise given by Jesus in Acts 1:5, "You will be baptized with the Holy Spirit not many days from now." This sign was clear enough so that all of those present for the Feast of Weeks were able to see that an impossible event was actually happening. The language speech in this chapter has a second, though subordinate, purpose—

the communication of the gospel to people of a foreign tongue. [10]

However, there was much labor to be done. Beginning in 36 C.E., with the conversion of Cornelius, an uncircumcised Gentile, the gospel got underway in its spread to non-Jewish people of every nation. (Acts, chap. 10) In truth, so swiftly did it spread that by about 60 C.E., the apostle Paul could say that the gospel had been "proclaimed in all creation that is under heaven." (Col. 1:23) Consequently, by the time of the last apostles death (John c. 100 C.E.), Jesus' faithful followers had made disciples all the way through the Roman Empire—in Asia, Europe, and Africa!

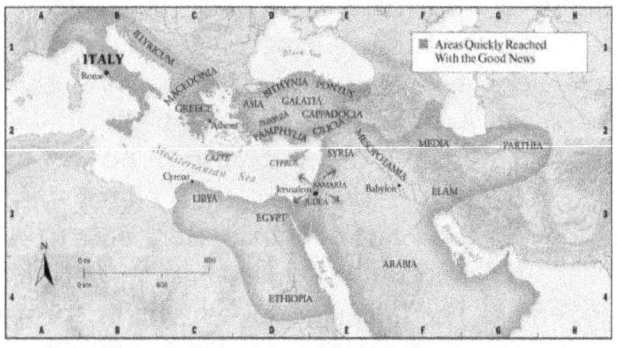

---

[10] Chad Brand, "Tongues, Gift Of", in Holman Illustrated Bible Dictionary, ed. Charles Draper, Archie England, Steve Bond et al., 1605 (Nashville, TN: Holman Bible Publishers, 2003).

Spread of Christianity in the first century[11]

Modern-day Speaking in Tongues

Among those 'speaking in tongues' today are Pentecostals and Baptists, also Roman Catholics, Episcopalians, Methodists, Lutherans, and Presbyterians. Jesus said, "When the Spirit of truth comes, he will guide you into all the truth ..." Would the Pentecostals or the Baptists, who "speak in tongues" suggest that the Roman Catholics, who "speak in tongues" have been 'guided into all the truth,' by the Holy Spirit, as well as the other way around. If modern-day "speaking in tongues" is truly, the same as the first century, and it is evidence proof that a person has Holy Spirit; then, all of the above groups would equally have to be the true path to God.

There is certainly mixed feeling over the revival of speaking in tongues at the beginning of the 20th century. Many see it as nothing more than excessiveness of unhinged persons, doing nothing more than drawing attention to themselves. On the other hand, many see it as the second Pentecost, identical to the

---

[11] (Ac 1:8; 2:1-4, 11; 2:37-41; Ac 5:27, 28, 40-42; 6:7; 8:1, 4, 14-17; 10:1-48; 11:20, 21)

occurrence of speaking with tongues in 33 C.E. There is a difference though for the modern-day counterpart where speaking in unknown tongues occurs. A rapturous explosion of jumbled sounds usually initiates it. Many who have been present at such occasions are unable to understand the chaotic speech, as is the case with all others who are present as well as the speaker himself.

Certainly, any reasonable person is moved to ask 'where the benefit in such unknown tongues is, and where the interpreters are?' It is true that there are some, who claim to interpret this incomprehensible speech, yet here again there exist credibility, because different explanations are offered for the same speech. In an attempt at removing this difficulty, they offer that God has simply given a different interpretation to these ones. However, they are unable to remove the stain that some of this speech has been base, degrading and depraved. Ronald E. Baxter, in his book *Charismatic Gift of Tongues*, mentions an example where a man refused to interpret the speech of a woman who spoke in the so-called 'gift of tongues,' saying, "The language was the vilest of the vile." This is hardly in harmony with the first-century Christian congregation, where tongues were used for "building up the church." 1 Corinthians 14:4-6, 12, 18.

Still, some have heard the interpretation of what they perceive to be a breathtaking message, and believe with their whole heart that God is using this unintelligible speech to give messages to his people. The only problem with this is that Muhammad, Joseph Smith and others make the same kind of argument. The book of Mormon is the supposed second testament of Christ for millions of Mormons. However, like the modern-day speaking in tongues, we are told very clearly to not go beyond what is written, do not add, nor take away, and that there would be no more miraculous messages until after Armageddon, where more books would be made available. Further still, what could be added by the unintelligible speech that is not available by means of Jesus Christ and the apostles through the Greek New Testament: "All Scripture is breathed out by God and profitable for teaching, for reproof, for correction, and for training in righteousness, that the man of God may be competent, equipped for every good work." 2 Timothy 3:16, 17; Deut. 4:12; Gal 1:8; Rev 20:12; 21:18, 19

As is quite clear from the New Testament itself, the gift of tongues was for a congregation that was in its infancy, and was needed for the preaching of the gospel and the building up the church. However, this is no longer the case: "But even if we or an angel from heaven should preach to you a gospel contrary ["at variance with," *The New English Bible*] to the one we preached to you, let him be accursed."—Galatians 1:8.

Thus then, the gift of tongues is no longer needed, and there is no Biblical foundation for supposing that it is an element of modern-day Christianity. In fact, it is unlikely that it ever survived to the middle of the second-century C.E. At present, the Bible is whole and extensively obtainable, and the Word of God is all that we require. This book alone is a road map to an approved relationship with the Father and the Son, which leads to life eternal. John 17:3; Revelation 22:18, 19

The primary verse to consider reads, "For one who speaks in a tongue speaks not to men but to God; for no one understands him, but he utters mysteries in the Spirit." (1 Cor. 14:2, ESV) When considering this verse, he should keep verses 13-19 of the same chapter in mind.

In other words, those who speak in a tongue speak to God as opposed to men **if** he does not have an interpreter for his speech that is to men who are listening. That is to say, the speaking in tongues is meaningless to the men listening, who do not know (understand) the foreign language as given miraculously through the Holy Spirit. It is for this very reason that Paul says, "no one understands." It could also have been that even the speaker himself of the foreign language did not understand what he was saying, because he was not also given the power to interpret (translate). Therefore, without an interpreter, be it himself or another, his speech would only be understood by God, i.e., would be speech only to God, as opposed to men. This is why the apostle Paul would say that if there were no interpreters present, the one speaking in a foreign tongue, should also pray for the gift of interpretation as well. This is so he can speak also to men in a beneficial manner, as well as bring praise to God.

It is Paul, in the first-century, who through the Corinthian congregation sat straight those who had become spellbound and awestruck with the gift of tongues, behaving juvenile, young in the Spirit. While the gift of tongues had its purpose, these ones acted as though it was the most important aspect of the Christian church. (1 Corinthians 14:1-39) The apostle Paul made several things very clear: it was not even a gift that all possessed. Moreover, it did not contribute as an identifying mark of a true Christian, or lead to salvation. Moreover, it was second to the gift of prophecy [proclaiming]. (Elwell, 2001, 1207) Therefore, this gift was not some marker that identified a person as a true Christian, nor was it required to receive the gift of life. 1 Corinthians 12:29, 30; 14:4, 5

What is the Real Force Behind Today's Speaking in Tongues?

There is no doubt that the charismatic church leaders of the 20th century are the impetus behind the resurgence of the speaking in tongues phenomena, pushing their flock members through emotionalism and coercion to achieve this alleged gift. This emotionalist duress is brought on by these church leaders, who exclude any who are unable to speak in tongues, and treat the other members of the church as superior for their ability to speak in tongues. Therefore, the motivating factor is not the Spirit, not to build up the church, not the glorification of God, but to belong.

Should Christians be identified by their ability to "speak in tongues"?

John 13:35 English Standard Version (ESV)

35 By this all people will know that you are my disciples, if you have love for one another."

1 Corinthians 13:1 English Standard Version (ESV)

¹ If I speak in the tongues of men and of angels, but have not love, I am a noisy gong or a clanging cymbal.

Jesus made the Great Commission all too clear when he said, you will receive power when the Holy Spirit has come upon you, and you will be my witnesses in Jerusalem and in all Judea and Samaria, and to the end of the earth." (Ac 1:8) He had instructed them and us to "Go therefore and make disciples of all nations, teaching them" (Matt 28:19-20). Moreover, he had earlier stressed that this was the last sign before the end of this age, by saying, "this gospel of the kingdom will be proclaimed throughout the whole world as a testimony to all nations, and then the end will come." (Matt 24:14) Do we see this being done by the charismatic groups, who advocate "speaking in tongues"? When was the last time you saw a Pentecostal come to your door, proclaiming the Good News? When was the last time you were out, and a Pentecostal witnessed to you? What Pentecostal church have you ever been to that has an evangelism program, to train its members to evangelize their community?

This gift of tongues is possible by mass hysteria. Worse still, the spirit directing this movement may very well not be the Holy Spirit. "She followed Paul and us, crying out, these men are servants of the Most High God, who proclaim to you the way of salvation.' And this she kept doing for many days. Paul, having become greatly annoyed, turned and said to the spirit, 'I command you in the name of Jesus Christ to come out of her.' And it came out that very hour." (Acts 16:17, 18) The apostle Paul cautioned, "Satan disguises himself as an angel of light." (2 Corinthians 11:14) By seeking a Biblical gift that is no more, these ones have made themselves possible victims of "the lawless one [who] is by the activity of Satan with all power and false signs and wonders, and with all wicked deception for those who are perishing, because they refused to love the truth and so be saved." (2 Thessalonians 2:9, 10) However, some might ask:

Does not Mark 16:17, 18 (NKJ) show that the gift of 'speaking with new tongues' would be a sign, so as to recognize believers?

Mark 16:17-18 New King James Version (NKJV)

¹⁷ And these signs will follow those who believe: In My name they will cast out demons; **they will speak with new tongues**; ¹⁸ they will take up serpents; and if they drink anything deadly, it will by no means hurt them; they will lay hands on the sick, and they will recover."

First, there is the telling fact that two of the oldest and most highly respected Bible manuscripts, the Vaticanus 03 and the Sinaiticus 01, do not contain this section; they conclude Mark's Gospel with verse eight. This is true of the early versions as well: Syriac, Coptic, Armenian, and Georgian. The early church fathers, Clement, Origen, Cyprian, and Cyril of Jerusalem had no knowledge of anything beyond verse eight. There is little wonder that the noted manuscript authority Dr. Westcott states, "the verses which follow [9-20] are no part of the original narrative but an appendage." Among other noted scholars of the same opinion are Tregelles, Tischendorf, Griesbach, Metzger, and Comfort, to mention just a few.

Adding weight to this evidence of the Greek manuscripts, versions and church fathers are the church historian Eusebius and the Bible translator Jerome. Eusebius wrote that the longer ending was not in the "accurate copies," for "at this point [verse 8] the end of the Gospel according to Mark is determined in nearly all the copies of the Gospel according to Mark." In addition, Jerome, writing about 407 C.E. said, "nearly all Greek MSS have not got this passage."

The vocabulary and style of Mark 16:9-20 vary so drastically from the Gospel of Mark that it scarcely seems possible that Mark himself wrote those verses. Mark's style is plain, direct; his paragraphs are short and the transitions are simple. However, in this ending, there is well-arranged succession of statements, each of them having proper introductory expressions.

Then there is the consideration of the vocabulary of Mark. Verses 9 through 20 contain words that do not appear elsewhere in Mark's Gospel, and some that do not appear in any of the Gospels, and some still that do not appear in the whole of the Greek New Testament. Verses 9 through 20 contain 163 Greek words, of which, 19 words, 2 phrases do not occur elsewhere in the Gospel of Mark. Looking at it another way, in these 12 verses there are 109 different words, and, of these, 11 words and 2 phrases are exclusive to these 12 verses. Moreover, the doctrinal thesis of Joseph Hug showed that when compared with the vocabulary of the other Gospels, the Apostolic Fathers, and the apocryphal literature, you have 12 verses in "an advanced state of tradition." The note at the end of Metzger's The Text of the New Testament, where I found a summary of Hug's thesis, states:

> The vocabulary suggests that the composition of the ending is appropriately located at the end of the first century or in the middle of the second century. Those who were responsible for adding the verses were intent, not only to supply a suitable ending for the Second Gospel, but also to provide missionary instruction to a Christian Hellenistic community that participated in charismatic activities... (Metzger 1964, 1968, 1992, 297)

The content of these verses also remove them from being considered as original. There is nothing within the whole of the New Testament, which would support the contention in verse 18 that the disciples of Christ were able to drink poison, having no harm come to them. In addition, within this spurious text, you have eleven apostles refusing to believe the testimony of two disciples whom

Jesus had come across on the way and to whom he made himself known. However, when the two disciples found the eleven, their reaction was quite different, stating, "The Lord has risen indeed, and has appeared to Simon!" Luke 24:13-35

In summary, Mark 16:9-20 **(1)** is not found in two of the oldest and most highly regarded Greek manuscripts as well as others. **(2)** They are also not found in many of the oldest versions. **(3)** The early church fathers had no knowledge of anything beyond verse eight. **(4)** Such ancient scholars as Eusebius and Jerome marked them spurious. **(5)** The style of these verses is utterly different from that of Mark. **(6)** The vocabulary used in these verses is different from that of Mark. **(7)** Verse 8 does not transition well with verse 9, jumping from the women disciples to Jesus' resurrection appearance. Jesus does not need to appear because Mark ended with the announcement that he had. We only want that because the other Gospels give us an appearance. So we expect it. **(8)** The very content of these verses contradicts the facts and the rest of the Greek New Testament. With textual scholarship, being very well aware of Mark's abrupt style of writing, and abrupt ending to his Gospel does not seem out of place. Eusebius and Jerome, as well as this writer, agree.

Mark 16:17-18 New King James Version (NKJV)

¹⁷ And these signs will follow those who believe: In My name **(1)** they will cast out demons; **(2)** they will speak with new tongues; **(3)** ¹⁸ they will take up serpents; and if they drink anything deadly, it will by no means hurt them; **(4)** they will lay hands on the sick, and they will recover."

Is this really, what the Bible teaches?

While Paul was bitten by a poisonous snake and survived, we never find anyone in the New

Testament going out to find poisonous snakes, for the purpose of handling them in a religious service. To the contrary, Paul quickly shook off the poisonous snake that had attached itself to his hand. One must ask, 'what purpose would religious snake handling have?' All of the gifts that were bestowed on the first century Christians had a practical purpose. The number one purpose was to evidence to the Jews that the Israelite nation was no longer the way to God, faith in Jesus Christ was.

As for Tongues, They Will Cease

Some may argue that the evidence does not give one any idea of when the gift of tongues was to end. However, they would be mistaken in this case. There are three lines of evidence that present the fact that the gift of tongues would die out shortly after the death of the last apostle, which was the apostle John, who died about 98-100 C.E. **First**, the gift of tongues was always passed on to the person, only by an apostle: either by laying his hands on this one, or at least being present. (Acts 2:4, 14, 17; 10:44-46; 19:6; see also Acts 8:14-18.) **Second**, 1 Corinthians 13:8 informed the Corinthian reader specifically that this gift would "cease." In short, the Greek word for cease [*pausontai*], means to 'peter out,' or 'to die out,' not to be brought to a halt. We will deal with *pausontai* more extensively in a moment. **Third**, both one and two are exactly what happened when we look at the history of this gift of tongues. M'Clintock and Strong's *Cyclopaedia* (Vol. VI, p. 320) says that it is "an uncontested statement that during the first hundred years after the death of the apostles we hear little or nothing of the working of miracles by the early Christians." Therefore, following their passing off the scene and after those who in that way had obtained the gift of tongues breathed their last breath; the gift of tongues should have died out with these ones. (Elwell, 2001, 1207-8) This analysis concurs with the intention of those gifts as acknowledged at Hebrews 2:2-4.

Daniel B. Wallace in his *Greek Grammar Beyond the Basics* helps us to better comprehend how we are to understand *pausontai* of 1 Corinthians 13:8:

> If the voice of the verb here is significant, then Paul is saying either that tongues will cut themselves off (direct middle) or, more likely, cease of their own accord, i.e., 'die out' without an intervening agent (indirect middle). It may be significant with reference to prophecy and knowledge, Paul used a different verb ([katargeo]) and out it in

the passive voice. In vv 9-10, the argument continues: 'for we *know* in part and we *prophecy* in part; but when the perfect comes, the partial shall be done away with [katargethesontai].' Here again, Paul uses the same passive verb he had used with prophecy and knowledge and he speaks of the verbal counterpart to the nominal 'prophecy' and 'knowledge.' Yet he does not speak about *tongues* being done away 'when the perfect comes.' The implication *may* be that tongues were to have 'died out' on their own *before* the perfect comes. (Wallace 1996, 422)

Speaking in Tongues and Today's Christianity

The gift of tongues "in the NT has three functions: to show the progress of the gift of the Spirit to the various people groups in the book of Acts in a salvation-history context, as a way of revealing the content of the NT revelation, and as a means of communicating cross-linguistically."[12] The apostle Paul made it

---

[12] Chad Brand, "Tongues, Gift Of", in Holman Illustrated Bible Dictionary, ed. Charles Draper, Archie

abundantly clear that the interpretation must be clear and understood for the benefit of all, not the glorification of one. (1 Corinthians 14:26-33) Paul gave a warning: "So with yourselves, if with your tongue you utter speech that is not intelligible, how will anyone know what is said? For you will be speaking into the air." 1 Corinthians 14:9

It is true that many of the early Christians received this gift of tongues by way of Holy Spirit, which did *not* bring forth speech that was incomprehensible or untranslatable nonsense. In accord with Paul's advice, the Holy Spirit made available speech that brought about an outcome in the gospel being "preached in all creation under heaven."—Colossians 1:23.

The church has been attempting with great vigor, to fulfill, Jesus Christ's command of "the gospel must first be proclaimed to all nations." (Mark 13:10) The same as was the case in the first-century, all nations are required to take notice of the message of the ransom death, resurrection and ascension of Christ. This is achievable for the reason that God's Word has now been translated into over 2,300 languages. The unchanged Spirit that instilled the first

---

England, Steve Bond et al., 1606 (Nashville, TN: Holman Bible Publishers, 2003).

Christians to speak in tongues is now sustaining the immense and extraordinary commission of the present-day church. 2 Timothy 1:13

Final Thoughts

Certainly, no writer wishes to be arrogantly dogmatic about a belief, an understanding of Scripture that could be overturned or adjusted before his eyes, as he grows in knowledge and understanding. The evidence seems to say that the gift of tongues was given to some in the infant Christian congregation to establish it as the new way to God, to give witness to the mighty acts of God that include the ransom sacrifice of Christ, his resurrection and ascension, and to communicate rapidly to those who spoke other languages.

These abilities were only established by the presence or lying on of hands by the apostles. This coincides with 1 Corinthians 13:8 and the history of these phenomena. Our Greek word for "cease" means that the gift of tongues was to 'die out' over time as the last of those who had received this gift passed off the scene of this earth. This is established by the historical fact that the second century saw just that being evidenced. Today, the Christian is moved by Spirit to speak with his heart and mind, defending and establishing the gospel, and destroying false doctrines, snatching some back from the fire. It is these things, which will give credence to the words of the modern-day Christian congregation: "God is really among you." 1 Corinthians 14:24, 25

BASIC TEACHING: Do We Have a Soul that Is Apart From Us?

Many have wondered what happens to the soul after death. Do humans have a soul that is apart from them? What is the soul? Is the soul, some invisible force within us, which survives after death? While this seems farfetched to some, many believe this to be true. Many have heard the claims on television, in book and magazines, about those, who claim they have had so-called life-after-death experiences. Here is a question for you as a reader, before we look at the first Bile verse, 'Does the soul breathe to stay alive?' Likely, most would answer, "No." Let us see what the Bible says.

A Soul Breathes

Genesis 2:7 American Standard Version (ASV)

⁷ And Jehovah God formed man of the dust of the ground, and breathed into his nostrils the breath of life; and man became a living soul.

Human soul = body **[dust of the ground]** + active life force **("spirit") [Hebrew, ruach]** within the trillions of human cells which make up the human body + breath of life [Hebrew, neshamah] that sustains the life force from God.

Genesis 2:7 tells us that God formed man out of the "dust of the ground". In other words, he was formed from the elements of the soil. This body needed life and so Jehovah caused the trillions of cells in his body to come to life, giving him the force of life. Ruach "spirit" is the active life force that Adam now possessed. However, for this life force to continue to feed these trillions of cells, there needed to be oxygen, sustained by the breathing. Therefore, we all know what God did next: he "breathed into his nostrils the breath [neshamah] of life." At this point Adam's lungs would sustain the breathing the life force into those body cells.

If we are to understand fully what the "soul" is, we must investigate what the Hebrew and Greek words mean. The Hebrew word translated "soul" is *ne'phesh*. What does "nephesh" mean? The *Holman Illustrated Bible Dictionary* says,

> In the Hebrew OT, the word generally translated "soul" is *nephesh*. The word occurs over 750 times, and it means primarily "life" or "possessing life." It is used of both

animals ([Gen. 9:12](); [Ezek. 47:9]()) and humans ([Gen. 2:7]()). The word sometimes indicates the whole person, as for instance in [Gen. 2:7]() where God breathes breath (*neshamah*) into the dust and thus makes a "soul" (*nephesh*). A similar usage is found in [Gen. 12:5]() where Abram takes all the "souls" (persons) who were with him in Haran and moves on to Canaan. Similarly in [Num. 6:6]() it is used as a synonym for the body—the Nazirite is not to go near a dead *nephesh* ([Lev. 7:21](); [Hag. 2:13]()). (Brand, Draper and Archie 2003, 1523)

Soul as "a living creature"

The American Standard Version has our literal rendering of nephesh at Genesis 2:7, "and man became **a** living **soul**." The English Standard Version offers an interpretation of nephesh, "and the man became **a** living **creature**." (LEB same) The Holman Christian Standard Bible offers an interpretation of nephesh, "and the man became **a** living **being**." (NASB same) You will notice that Genesis 2:7 makes it all too clear that Adam was not given a soul, he does not have a soul, but that he became a living soul, i.e., a living creature, a living being. Therefore, the "soul" is a person, a creature, a being, not what we have. When we look at the Hebrew Old Testament using a literal rendering, this is born out.

Leviticus 5:1 New American Standard Bible (NASB)

5 'Now **if a** person [nephesh, **soul**] **sins** after he hears a public adjuration *to testify* when he is a witness, whether he has seen or *otherwise* known, if he does not tell *it*, then he will bear his guilt.

Leviticus 23:30 New American Standard Bible (NASB)

30 As for **any** person [nephesh, **soul**] **who does any work** on this same day, that person I will destroy from among his people.

Deuteronomy 24:7 Lexham English Bible (LEB)

7 "If a man is *caught* **kidnapping** somebody [nephesh, **a soul**] from *among* his countrymen, the *Israelites*, and he treats him as a slave or he sells him, then that kidnapper shall die, and *so* you shall purge the evil *from among you*.

Judges 16:16 New American Standard Bible (NASB)

¹⁶ It came about when she pressed him daily with her words and urged him, that his **soul was annoyed** to death.

Job 19:2 Updated American Standard Version (UASV)

² How long will you **torment my soul**, And break me in pieces with words?

Psalm 119:28 New American Standard Bible (NASB)

²⁸ My **soul weeps** because of grief; Strengthen me according to Your word.

We notice here in the above verses that a soul sins, a soul works, a soul can be kidnapped, a soul can get annoyed, a soul can be tormented, and a soul can weep. These things happened to a person, to a creature, to a being, not to an inanimate object within the human body, which is supposed lives on after death. The *Holman Illustrated Bible Dictionary* says,

> **New Testament** Greek word *psuche* carries many of the same meanings as the Hebrew *nephesh*. Often the soul is equated with the total person. Romans 13:1 says, "Everyone [soul] must submit to the governing authorities" equating "soul" (one) with

"person" (cp. Acts 2:41; 3:23). There will be "affliction and distress for every human being [soul] who does evil, first to the Jew, and also to the Greek" (Rom. 2:9 HCSB). Soul in the NT also indicates the emotions or passions: "But the Jews who refused to believe stirred up and poisoned the minds [*psuche*] of the Gentiles against the brothers" (Acts 14:2 HCSB). In John 10:24 the Jews asked Jesus, "How long are You going to keep us [our souls] in suspense?" Jesus also told the disciples that they should love God with all of their souls (Mark 12:30), indicating something of the energy and passion that ought to go into loving Him. (Brand, Draper and Archie 2003, 1523)

When we look at the Greek New Testament using a literal rendering, "soul," the basic idea inherent in the word as the Bible writers used it, namely, that it is a living person, a living creature, or a living being; or, the life that a person or an animal has as a soul.

John 12:27 New American Standard Bible (NASB)

²⁷ "Now **My soul has become troubled**; and what shall I say, 'Father, save Me from this hour'? But for this purpose I came to this hour.

Acts 2:43 American Standard Version (ASV)

⁴³ And **fear came upon every soul**: and many wonders and signs were done through the apostles.

Romans 13:1 New American Standard Bible (NASB)

13 Every person [*psuche*, **soul**] is **to be in subjection** to the governing authorities. For there is no authority except from God, and those which exist are established by God.

1 Thessalonians 5:14 Lexham English Bible (LEB)

¹⁴ And we urge you, brothers, admonish the disorderly, console the **discouraged** [oligo*psuche*, literally "those of little **soul**," i.e., "discouraged."], help the sick, be patient toward all *people*.

1 Peter 3:20 New American Standard Bible (NASB)

²⁰ who once were disobedient, when the patience of God kept waiting in the days of Noah, during the construction of the ark, in

which a few, that is, eight persons [*psuchai*, **souls**], were brought safely through *the* water.

We notice here in the above verses that a soul can become troubled, fear can come upon a soul, a soul is to be in subjection to the governmental authorities, a soul can get discouraged, and souls can be delivered through a flood. These things happen to a person, a creature, a being, not an inanimate object within the human body, which supposed lives on after death. We note to from our quote of the Holman Illustrated Bible Dictionary, animals are "souls" too.

Genesis 1:24	**Numbers 31:28**
American Standard Version (ASV)	American Standard Version (ASV)
24 And God said, Let the earth bring forth living creatures [nephesh, soul] after their kind, cattle, and creeping things, and beasts of the earth after their kind: and it was so.	28 And levy a tribute unto Jehovah of the men of war that went out to battle: one soul of five hundred, both of the persons, and of the oxen, and of the asses, and of the flocks:

Soul as the Life of the Creature

"Soul" is used in Scripture as reference to the life that a living person, a living creature, a living animal has. This does not negate what we learned in the above. We are living "souls," i.e., living persons. It does not change a thing to use "soul" in the sense of our possessing "life." Below are a few examples.

Exodus 4:19 American Standard Version (ASV)

¹⁹ And Jehovah said to Moses in Midian, "Go, return into Egypt, for all the men are dead who sought your life **[nephesh, soul]**."

Joshua 9:24 American Standard Version (ASV)

²⁴ And they answered Joshua, and said, Because it was certainly told thy servants, how that Jehovah your God commanded his servant Moses to give you all the land, and to destroy all the inhabitants of the land from before you; therefore we feared greatly for our lives **[nephesh, souls]** because of you, and have done this thing.

2 Kings 7:7 American Standard Version (ASV)

⁷ Wherefore they arose and fled in the twilight, and left their tents, and their horses, and their asses, even the camp as it was, and fled for their life **[nephesh, soul]**.

Proverbs 12:10 American Standard Version (ASV)

¹⁰ A righteous man regards the life **[nephesh, soul]** of his beast; But the tender mercies of the wicked are cruel.

Matthew 20:28 American Standard Version (ASV)

²⁸ even as the Son of man came not to be ministered to, but to minister, and to give his life **[psuche, soul]** a ransom for many.

Philippians 2:30 New American Standard Bible (NASB)

³⁰ because he came close to death for the work of Christ, risking his life **[psuche, soul]** to complete what was deficient in your service to me.

Now, we do not want to misrepresent the *Holman Illustrated Bible Dictionary*, by quoting two paragraphs, where this author would agree, and not go on to the next paragraph, where they would disagree with this author. There are two positions, when it comes to the biblical position of the body and the soul. **We**

would disagree with the first, which is "**holistic dualism**—that there is a difference between body and soul, but the two are linked together by God such that humans are not complete when the two are separated." Our position that **we would agree** with, would be the second, which is the "**monistic view** that the soul is not separable from the body at all. Nearly all who have held the second view have also believed that after death Christians 'go to sleep' and await the resurrection." (Bold mine) The Holman Illustrated Bible Dictionary holds to the holistic dualism position, as they write,

> It is also the case that the NT speaks of the soul as something that is distinguishable from the physical existence of a person. Jesus made this point when He observed, "Don't fear those who kill the body but are not able to kill the soul; but rather, fear Him who is able to destroy both soul and body in hell" (Matt. 10:28 HCSB). James seems to have the same thing in mind when he concludes his letter, "He should know that whoever turns a sinner from the error of his way will save his life [soul] from death" (James 5:20 HCSB; cp. Rev. 6:9; 20:4). This may be the idea found in Mark 8:36,

"For what does it benefit a man to gain the whole world yet lose his life [soul]?" (HCSB). Scripture clearly teaches that persons continue to exist consciously after physical death. Jesus pointed out that as the God of Abraham, Isaac, and Jacob, He is the God of the living. These still live, their souls having returned to God (Eccles. 12:7). (Brand, Draper and Archie 2003, 1523)

We will take their texts one at a time, offering the text, and then offering a thought that will clarify what was meant by the author.

Matthew 10:28 Holman Christian Standard Bible (HCSB)

28 Don't fear those who kill the body but are not able to kill the soul; rather, fear Him who is able to destroy both soul and body in hell.[13]

What is meant by this is, man can kill the body alone, but he cannot kill "life," as in everlasting life. The prospect of life is in the

---

[13] For a discussion of the hellfire doctrine, please see, **BASIC TEACHINGS OF THE BIBLE Life Questions Christians Ask Themselves and Others** by Andrews, Edward D. (Nov 28, 2013)

hands of God alone. He can kill both the body, which is used to represent what we have here and now, but he can also kill any prospect that we have at everlasting life. Again, man can kill the body; they cannot kill the person for an eternity, as the hope of a resurrection is in hands of God.

James 5:20 Holman Christian Standard Bible (HCSB)

[20] let him know that whoever turns a sinner from the error of his way will save his life **[soul]** from death and cover a multitude of sins.

First, we should point out that, the 'life **[soul]** that is saved from death' is, not the one doing the helping, but rather, it is the sinner. Our works do not save us; we are saved by the loving-kindness of God, in offering his Son as a ransom sacrifice for all, who trust in that sacrifice. (Acts 4:12) The person who was saved was walking down the path of eternal death, from where there is no hope for eternal life. When the one Christian helped the sinner turn back from his error, by spreading love and counsel, as well as prayer, he helped this sinner stay on the path of life, eternal life, by way of the atonement sacrifice of Christ.

Mark 8:36 Holman Christian Standard Bible (HCSB)

³⁶ For what does it benefit a man to gain the whole world yet lose his life **[soul]**?

Here again, it is not referring to the person's life in this present imperfect age, but eternal life that is to come after Jesus brings the last enemy to nothing, death. We will deal with Ecclesiastes 12:7 below.

Can the Soul Die?

When we die, what happens to the soul? If you recall from above that the "soul" is the person, the being, the creature, i.e., us, and the **life** that we have. If you recall from above, the **Human soul** = body **[dust of the ground]** + active life force **("spirit") [Hebrew, ruach]** within the trillions of human cells which make up the human body + breath of life [Hebrew, neshamah] that sustains the life force from God. In other words, the "soul" is we as a whole, everything that we are, so the soul or we humans can die. Let us look at a few verses, which make that all too clear.

Ecclesiastes 3:19-20 New American Standard Bible (NASB)

¹⁹ For the fate of the sons of men [humans or people] and the fate of beasts is the same. As one dies so dies the other; indeed, they all have the same breath and there is no advantage for man over beast, for all is vanity. ²⁰ All go to the same place. All came from the dust and all return to the dust.

In other words, when we breathe our last breath, our cells begin to die. Death is the ending of all vital functions or processes in an organism or cell. When our heart stops beating, our blood is no longer circulating, carrying nourishment and oxygen (by breathing) to the billions of cells in our body; we are what are termed, clinically dead. However, somatic death has yet to occur, meaning we can be revived, after many minutes, if the heart and lungs can be restarted again, which gives the cells the oxygen they need.

After about three minutes of clinical death, the brain cells begin to die, meaning the chances of reviving the person is less likely as each second passes. We know that it is vital that the breathing and blood flow be maintained for the life force (*ruach chaiyim*) in the cells. Nevertheless, it is not the lack of breathing or the failure of the heart beating alone, but rather the active life force **("spirit") [Hebrew, ruach]** within the trillions of human cells which make up the human body + breath of life [Hebrew, neshamah] that sustains the life force from God.

Psalm 104:29	Psalm 146:4	Ecclesiastes 8:8
English Standard Version (ESV)	English Standard Version (ESV)	English Standard Version (ESV)
[29] When you hide your face, they are dismayed; when you take away their breath, they die and return to their dust.	[4] When his breath departs, he returns to the earth; on that very day his plans perish.	[8] No man has power to retain the spirit, or power over the day of death. There is no discharge from war, nor will wickedness deliver those who are given to it.

Again, …

Ezekiel 18:4	Leviticus 21:1	Numbers 6:6
English Standard	American Standard	American Standard

Version (ESV)	Version (ASV)	Version (ASV)
⁴ Behold, all souls are mine; the soul of the father as well as the soul of the son is mine: the soul who sins shall die.	**21** And Jehovah said to Moses, Speak to the priests, the sons of Aaron, and say to them, There shall none defile himself for the dead **[Or "for a soul."]** among his people;	⁶ All the days that he separates himself unto Jehovah he shall not come near to a dead body **[Or "soul."]**.

Again, the death of a "soul" means the death of a person ...

1 Kings 19:4	**Jonah 4:8**	**Mark 3:4**
American Standard Version (ASV)	American Standard Version (ASV)	American Standard Version (ASV)
⁴ But he himself went a day's journey into the	⁸ And it came to pass, when the sun arose, that God	⁴ And he said to them, Is it lawful on the sabbath day

wilderness, and came and sat down under a juniper-tree: and he requested for himself that he **[Or "his soul.]** "might die, and said, It is enough; now, O Jehovah, take away my life [soul]; for I am not better than my fathers.	prepared a sultry east wind; and the sun beat upon the head of Jonah, that he fainted, and requested for himself that he might die **[Or "that his soul might die."]**, and said, It is better for me to die than to live.	to do good, or to do harm? to save a life **[Or "soul."]**, or to kill? But they held their peace.

As you can see from the above texts, a "soul," or person can die. However, how are we to understand those texts that say the "soul" went out of a person, or came back into a person?

Soul Departing and Soul Coming into a Person

Genesis 35:18 English Standard Version (ESV)

¹⁸ And as her soul was departing (for she was dying), she called his name Ben-oni; but his father called him Benjamin.

Are we to understand from this that Rachel had some inner being, a soul, which departed from her at death? No. You will recall from the texts from above that the term "soul" can also be used in reference to the life one has. Thus, this is a reference to her life that she had leaving her. Note the *Lexham English Bible*, "And it happened *that* when **her <u>life</u> was departing** (for she was dying), she called his name Ben-Oni. But his father called him Benjamin." (Bold and underline is mine) Therefore, it was her "life" that she had, which departed from her, not some inner being.

1 Kings 17:22 American Standard Version (ASV)

²² And Jehovah listened to the voice of Elijah; and the soul of the child came into him again, and he revived.

Here again, the word "soul" is the "life" that someone has. The *New American Standard*

Bible reads, "The **life** of the child returned to him and he revived." The *Lexham English Bible* reads, "The **life** of the child returned within him, and he lived." The *Holman Christian Standard Bible* reads, "The boy's **life** returned to him, and he lived." (Bold is mine)

John 11:11 English Standard Version (ESV)	**1 Kings 2:10** English Standard Version (ESV)
¹¹ After saying these things, he said to them, "Our friend Lazarus has fallen asleep, but I go to awaken him."	¹⁰ Then David slept with his fathers and was buried in the city of David.

Notice that Lazarus' death is equated with being asleep in death, while King David is referred to as sleeping in death. This gives the reader a hope, as just as easily as you and I can awaken a person from sleep, Jesus is going to awaken people from death, a death like sleep. We are going to look at these verses a little differently that we have with the others. We will pause for a moment to see how a literal translation is best (which has already been demonstrated), with an interpretation in a footnote. Moreover, it is important that we read those footnotes. Otherwise, we can come to the wrong conclusions.

Excursion   Literal   versus   Dynamic Equivalent

1   Kings   2:10   Essentially   Literal Translation (ASV, RSV, ESV, NASB)

And <u>David slept</u> with his fathers, and was buried in the city of David.

And <u>David slept</u> with his fathers, and was buried in the city of David.

Then <u>David slept</u> with his fathers and was buried in the city of David.

Then <u>David slept</u> with his fathers and was buried in the city of David.

1   Kings   2:10   Though-for-Thought Translation (GNB, CEV, NLT, MSG)

<u>David died</u> and was buried in David's City.

Then <u>he died</u> and was buried in Jerusalem.

Then <u>David died</u> and was buried with his ancestors in the City of David.

Then <u>David joined his ancestors</u>. He was buried in the City of David.

One could conclude that the thought-for-thought translations are conveying the idea in a more clear and immediate way, but is this really the case? There are three points that are missing from the thought-for-thought translation:

In the scriptures, "sleep" is used metaphorically as death, also inferring a temporary state where one will wake again, or be resurrected. That idea is lost in the thought-for-thought translation. (Ps 13:3; John 11:11-14; Ac 7:60; 1Co 7:39; 15:51; 1Th 4:13)

David's sleeping with or lying down with his father also conveys the idea of having closed his life and having found favor in God's eyes as did his forefathers.

When we leave out some of the words from the original, we also leave out the possibility of more meaning being drawn from the text. Missing is the word *shakab* ("to lie down" or "to sleep"), *'im* ("with") and *'ab* in the plural ("forefathers").

Psalm 13:3 (American Standard Version)

Consider *and* answer me, O Jehovah my God: Lighten mine eyes, lest I sleep the *sleep of* death

John 11:11-14 (American Standard Version)

After saying these things, he said to them, "Our friend Lazarus is fallen asleep; but I go, that I may awake him out of sleep." The disciples therefore said to him, Lord, if he is fallen asleep, he will recover. Now Jesus had spoken of his death: but they thought that he spoke of taking rest in sleep. Then Jesus therefore said to them plainly, Lazarus is dead.

Acts 7:60 (American Standard Version)

And he kneeled down, and cried with a loud voice, Lord, lay not this sin to their charge. And when he had said this, he fell asleep.

1 Corinthians 7:39 (Updated American Standard Version)

A wife is bound as long as her husband lives. But if her husband should sleep (*koimethe*) [in death], she is free to be married to whom she wishes, only in the Lord.[14]

---

[14] The ASV, ESV, NASB, and other literal translation do not hold true to their literal translation philosophy here. This does not bode well in their claim that literal renderings are to be preferred. I am speaking primarily to the ESV translators, who make this claim in numerous books.

1 Corinthians 15:51 (American Standard Version)

Behold, I tell you a mystery: We all shall not sleep, but we shall all be changed,

1 Thessalonians 4:13 (American Standard Version)

But we would not have you ignorant, brethren, concerning them that fall asleep; that ye sorrow not, even as the rest, who have no hope.

Those who argue for a though-for-thought translation will say the literal translation "slept" or "lay down" is no longer a way of expressing death in the modern English speaking world. While this may be true to some extent, the context of chapter two, verse 1: ""when David was about to die" and the latter half of 2:10: "was buried in the city of David" really resolves that issue. Moreover, while the reader may have to meditate a little longer, or indulge him/herself in the culture of different Biblical times, they will not be deprived of the full potential that a verse has to convey. (Translating Truth, Grudem, Ryken, Collins, Polythress, & Winter, 2005, 21-22) Therefore, we offer a word of caution here. The dynamic equivalent can and does obscure things from the reader by overreaching in their translations.

His Spirit Goes Forth and He Returns to the Earth

Psalm 146:4 Young's Literal Translation (YLT)

⁴ His spirit goes forth; he returns to his earth, In that day have his thoughts perished.

Are we to understand that there is some spiritual being within us, which then departs from us at death? No, this is not the understanding, as the Psalmist next words were, "In that day have his thoughts perished," ("all his thinking ends," *NEB*). How, then, are we to understand this verse?

In the Hebrew Scriptures, you have ruach, and in the Greek New Testament, you have pneuma, both basically meaning "breath." This is why other translations read, "His breath goes forth."

Psalm 146:4	Psalm 146:4	Psalm 146:4
English Standard Version (ESV)	Lexham English Bible (LEB)	Holman Christian Standard Bible (HCSB)
⁴ When his **breath departs**, he returns to the	⁴ His **breath departs**; he returns to his plot;	⁴ When his **breath leaves** him,

| earth; on that very day his plans perish. | on that day his plans perish. | he returns to the ground; on that day his plans die. |

You will notice this further clarified, when Moses informs us of what took place at the flood. However, we look at the literal translations first, followed by other literal translations that choose to define the use of the term "spirit." Not how we will use a footnote in the literal, and the others that chose to define.

Genesis 7:22	**Genesis 7:22**	**Genesis 7:22**
New American Standard Bible (NASB) ²² of all that was on the dry land, all in whose nostrils was the breath of the spirit of life **[breath of life]**, died.	American Standard Version (ASV) ²² all in whose nostrils was the breath of the spirit of life **[breath of life]**, of all that was on the dry land, died.	Young's Literal Translation (YLT) ²² all in whose nostrils [is] breath of a living spirit **[breath of life]** -- of all that [is] in the dry land -- have died.

Other literal and semi-literal translations,

Genesis 7:22	**Genesis 7:22**	**Genesis 7:22**
English Standard Version (ESV)	Lexham English Bible (LEB)	New Revised Standard Version (NRSV)
²² Everything on the dry land in whose nostrils was the breath of life **["a breath of spirit of life"]** died.	²² Everything in whose nostrils *was the breath of life* **["a breath of spirit of life"]**, among all that *was* on dry land, died.	²² everything on dry land in whose nostrils was the breath of life **["a breath of spirit of life"]** died.

Therefore, "ruach" and "pneuma," i.e., "spirit" can refer to the breath of life that is active with in both human and animal creatures. Then how do we explain Ecclesiastes 12:7?

Ecclesiastes 12:7 English Standard Version (ESV)

⁷ and the dust returns to the earth as it was, and the spirit returns to God who gave it.

Are we to understand that a spiritual being within us, leaves us at death, and returns to God? No. We just learned that the "spirit" is the "breath of life," which sustains human and animal life. Once we lose our "breath of life," and dare dead, the only hope of having it restored come from God. Therefore, "the spirit returns to God," in that our only hope for living again, but this time for eternally, comes from God. It is only God, who can restore the "breath of life," which enables us to live again. Keep in mind too, this person was never in heaven with God, so the idea of him as a spirit person returning to God is not what is meant. How can he return to God, if he was never in heaven with God to begin with? Again, it is the "breath of life," which enables the person to live that returns to God, not literally, but in the sense of his having the power to restore it.

Ecclesiastes 12:7	Ecclesiastes 12:7
Lexham English Bible (LEB)	New Revised Standard Version (NRSV)
7 And the dust returns to the earth as it was, and the breath returns to God who gave it.	**7** and the dust returns to the earth as it was, and the breath returns to God who gave it.

BASIC TEACHING: Does Abortion Show Respect for Life?

"Pro-life groups are optimistic about the effectiveness of ultrasound technology in persuading pregnant women to choose giving birth over having an abortion. Ultrasound technology has played an important role in helping pregnant women realize that the fetuses they carry are "alive and vulnerable.'"[15] At conception, according to the Bible, we are talking about as a living, human soul. (Genesis 2:7) Truly conservative Christians do not set aside the one person, the Creator, who is "the fountain of life." (Psalm 36:9) Below are the words of the Creator of life.

Genesis 25:22-23 American Standard Version (ASV)

22 And the children struggled together within her. And she said, If it be so, wherefore do I live? And she went to inquire of Jehovah. **23** And Jehovah said to her, Two nations are in thy womb, And two peoples shall be separated from thy bowels. And the one people shall be

---

[15] http://www.christianpost.com/news/ultrasound-technology-an-effective-piece-of-the-pro-life-message-88721/

stronger than the other people. And the elder shall serve the younger.

Notice here that God was well aware of the very personalities of these two boys, Jacob and Esau, even before their birth. Some 1,800 years later, one of God's angels informed Zechariah that his wife Elizabeth were going to have a son, and that his name should be called John. This unborn baby boy would grow to be one of the most important persons within God's Word. He was to prepare the way for the Son of God, Jesus Christ. Even though John the Baptist, as he came to be known, was a great man, his commission called for humility like no other in Scripture. He was to carry out a work that never gave any promotion or recognition of self, but rather point to Jesus Christ and his coming ministry. God knew just the type of personality that John would possess, even when he was in the womb of Elizabeth.--Luke 1:8-17

The Human Fetus

Psalm 139:13-16 English Standard Version (ESV)

[13] For you formed my inward parts;
 you **[God]** knitted me together in my mother's womb.

¹⁴ I praise you, for I am fearfully and wonderfully made.
Wonderful are your works;
   my soul knows it very well.
¹⁵ My frame was not hidden from you,
when I was being made in secret,
   intricately woven in the depths of the earth.
¹⁶ Your eyes saw my unformed substance;
in your book were written, every one of them,
   the days that were formed for me,
   when as yet there was none of them.

Acts 17:28 (ESV): "for 'In him [God] we live and move and have our being'"

Rom. 14:12 (ESV): "So then each of us will give an account of himself to God."

Are Unborn Children Worth Less in the Eyes of God?

Exodus 21:22-23 Updated American Standard Version (UASV)

²² "'And if men struggle with each other, and injure a pregnant woman, so that her child comes out [prematurely], and yet there is no **fatality** results [*ason*, Or "serious injury."]; he shall be surely fined, as the woman's husband shall lay upon him; and he shall pay as the judges determine. ²³ But if there is a **fatality** [*ason*], then he shall give life for life

Some translations like the *Revised Standard Version* below render the verses as though the woman is the main focus of the law. However, this just is not the case, as the Hebrew focuses on a serious injury or a fatality to either the mother or the child.

Exodus 21:22-23 Revised Standard Version (RSV)

²² "When men strive together, and hurt a woman with child, **so that there is a miscarriage**, and yet no harm follows, the one who hurt her **shall be fined**, according as the woman's husband shall lay upon him; and he shall pay as the judges determine. ²³ **If any harm follows**, then you shall give **life for life**

The picture that one could get from renderings like the RSV is that the only grave unease here is for the woman, not the unborn or premature child. Someone could determine from such a translation that if the hurt caused the death of a prematurely born child but no other harm to the woman, the guilty man was merely to receive a fine, as was the conclusion of Josephus of the first-century.

Here is how the first-century Jewish historian **Flavius Josephus** paraphrased these verses:

He that kicks a woman with child, so that the woman miscarry, let him pay a fine in money, as the judges shall determine, as having diminished the multitude by the destruction of what was in her womb; and let money also be given the woman's husband by him that kicked her; but if she die of the stroke, let him also be put to death, the law judging it equitable that life should go for life.[16]

Philo and others appear to have understood this law (Exod. 21:22, 25) better than Josephus, who seems to allow, that though the infant in the mother's womb, even after the mother were quick, and so the infant had a rational soul, were killed by the stroke upon the mother, yet if the mother escaped, the offender should only be fined, and not put to death; while the law seems rather to mean, that if the infant in that case be killed, though the mother escape, the offender must be put to death; and not only when the mother is killed, as Josephus

---

[16] Flavius Josephus and William Whiston, The Works of Josephus: Complete and Unabridged (Peabody: Hendrickson, 1996), Book IV, Chapter viii, paragraph 33.

understood it. It seems this was the exposition of the Pharisees in the days of Josephus.[17]

Alternatively, the translators of the Greek Septuagint Version of the Old Testament saw things differently.

Exodus 21:22-23 Septuagint Version of the Old Testament (LXX)

[22] And if two men strive and smite a woman with child, and her child be born imperfectly formed [or, "she miscarry of an embryo"], he shall be forced to pay a penalty: as the woman's husband may lay upon him, he shall pay with a valuation. [23] But if it be perfectly formed, he shall give life for life,[18]

Therefore, these translators believed that if what was miscarried were too young to have developed recognizable human features, a monetary fine would suffice. However, if the fetus was "perfectly formed" the man who gave cause to the loss of life of the prematurely born child must pay life for life. With such

---

[17] Ibid., footnote

[18] Lancelot Charles Lee Brenton, *The Septuagint Version of the Old Testament: English Translation* (London: Samuel Bagster and Sons, 1870), Ex 21:22–25.

disagreement going on, it is best that we go to the original Hebrew.

If you consider the possible outcomes, there are more than you may have thought. Let us look to the woman first. She could have suffered anything from a minor injury to a serious injury, even crippled, but no loss of life. Alternatively, she could have lost her life. Next, think of the child or children developing in her womb. If she was far enough along in her pregnancy, being struck could have brought about a premature birth. Then, there is the possible hurt of the unborn losing its life and the mother's hurt of having lost her child(ren). Clearly, the law had to cover a far range of outcomes.

Let us look at the law to see what it really said? Below is the literal rendering in the Hebrew-English Interlinear by Dr. G. R. Berry (read from right to left)

וְכִי־יִנָּצוּ֙ אֲנָשִׁ֔ים וְנָ֨גְפ֜וּ
And when contend men, and they strike

אִשָּׁ֤ה הָרָה֙ 22 וְיָצְא֣וּ יְלָדֶ֔יהָ
a woman 2 ¹pregnant, and goes forth her child,

וְלֹ֥א יִהְיֶ֖ה אָס֑וֹן עָנ֣וֹשׁ יֵעָנֵ֗שׁ
and not is injury; surely he shall be fined,

כַּֽאֲשֶׁ֨ר יָשִׁ֤ית עָלָיו֙ בַּ֣עַל
as may put upon him the husband of

הָֽאִשָּׁ֔ה וְנָתַ֖ן בִּפְלִלִֽים׃
the woman, and he shall give with the judges.

וְאִם־אָס֖וֹן יִהְיֶ֑ה וְנָתַתָּ֥ה נֶ֖פֶשׁ
And if injury is, (and) thou shalt give soul 23

תַּ֥חַת נָֽפֶשׁ׃
for soul,

The Hebrew word here rendered "injury" ("harm," Revised Standard Version) is *ason*. According to *The Hebrew and Aramaic Lexicon of the Old Testament*, ason means "fatal accident."[19] Therefore, the rendering "fatality" in the Updated American Standard Version allows one to understand more fully what the law had to say.

---

[19] Ludwig Koehler, Walter Baumgartner, M.E.J Richardson and Johann Jakob Stamm, The Hebrew and Aramaic Lexicon of the Old Testament, electronic ed. (Leiden; New York: E.J. Brill, 1999), 73.

The question that begs to be asked is, 'who is the term "fatality" applying to? It is to the mother alone, the child, or the mother and the child? The Jerusalem Bible reads:

Exodus 21:22-23 Jerusalem Bible (JB)

²² "'If, when men come to blows, they hurt a woman who is pregnant and she suffers a miscarriage, though *she* does not die of it, the man responsible must pay the compensation demanded of him, . . . ²³ But should *she* die, you shall give life for life. (Italics added)

The Jerusalem Bible is correct in the choice rendering of "fatality," but they go beyond translation into the realms of interpretation when they insert "she," which will cause the reader to believe that if the woman lost the child in a premature birth, but lived, the offender would only receive a fine. Is this really, what the Hebrew text says?

The above-mentioned interlinear reading discloses that the Hebrew does not limit the application of "injury" (fatality) to just the mother. Therefore, the *Commentary on the Old Testament* says that a fine was satisfactory only when "no injury [fatal accident] was done either to the woman or the child that was born." The commentary goes on to show that if what the Law merely meant was, if the mother lived, regardless of the child, only a fine would be imposed; then, the Hebrew text would have had the ending lah, "to her." Therefore, the verse would have read, 'When men struggle and they strike a pregnant woman and her child goes forth and no injury [fatality] is done to her, a fine must be paid.' Yet, the commentary concluded, "The omission of lah, also, apparently renders it impracticable to refer the words to [an] injury done to the woman alone."[20]

Hebrew scholar U. Cassuto (A Commentary on the Book of Exodus [Jerusalem: Magnes Press, 1967]) asserts, "The passage does not deal with miscarriage" (but is speaking of premature birth), thus assuming that the lxx rendering was conjectural and that the Hb. must and can be comprehended on its own. N. L. Collins points out that the verb used in 21:22 to refer to men fighting (.... from nṣh) always conveys the sense of two people fighting and thus the specificity in the lxx and Syriac translations (two men) is simply proper ancient translation and not the addition of a concept by periphrastic translators ("Notes on

---

[20] Carl Friedrich Keil and Franz Delitzsch, Commentary on the Old Testament. (Peabody, MA: Hendrickson, 2002).

the Text of Exodus XXI:22," VT 43 [1993]: 289–301).

The verses are about the sacredness of life, the life of the woman, or her unborn child. If the woman or her unborn child was seriously injured by a premature birth, or lost their life, the man would be punished to the degree of deliberateness and the circumstances. If there were no loss of life of either mother or child, there would be a fine. If there were a loss of life of either mother or child, there would be a death penalty.

The Hebrew word *yatsa*, has the following range of meaning, "to go out, come out; to bring out, lead forth; produce; to be brought out; emptied; by extension: to grow (of plants), to have offspring."[21] It is the word that is commonly used for giving birth in the Hebrew Old Testament, and "miscarriage" is a mistranslation. It should be noted that if Moses wanted to say "miscarriage," there was a Hebrew term for that, *shakol*. Finally, whether harm came to the child (*yeled*) or the mother, the punishment was the same.

---

[21] William D. Mounce, *Mounce's Complete Expository Dictionary of Old & New Testament Words* (Grand Rapids, MI: Zondervan, 2006), 951.

What is the Punishment for Taking a Human Life?

Gen. 9:6 (ESV): "Whoever sheds the blood of man, by man shall his blood be shed, for God made man in his own image."

1 John 3:15 (ESV): "no murderer has eternal life abiding in him."

Ex. 20:13 (ESV): "You shall not murder."

Early Christians on Abortion

The last apostle, John died about 98-100 C.E. Thereafter, you have church leaders, who became known as the Apostolic Fathers and the Apologists. While they are not inspired writers, they do convey the Christian mindset on abortion, right after the death of the apostles. Let us look at just a few out of many.

Barnabas 19:5 Epistle of Barnabas (c.70-130 C.E.)

⁵ You must not waver with regard to your decisions. "You shall not take the Lord's name in vain." You shall love your neighbor more than your own life. You shall not abort a child nor, again, commit infanticide. You must not withhold your hand from your son or your

daughter, but from their youth you shall teach them the fear of God.

Didache 2:1 The Teaching of the Twelve Apostles (c.80-140 C.E.)

[1] You shall not murder a child by abortion nor kill one who has been born.

Tertullian 9:8 Apology (c.197 C.E.)

[8] But with us murder is forbidden once and for all. We are not permitted to destroy even the foetus [fetus] in the womb, as long as blood is still being drawn to form a human being. To prevent the birth of a child is anticipated murder. It makes no difference whether one destroys a life already born or interferes with its coming to birth. One who will be a man is already one.

Basil: Letter to Amphilochius (347 C.E.)

"She who has deliberately destroyed a foetus has to pay the penalty of murder. And any hair-splitting distinction as to whether the foetus was formed or unformed is inadmissible to us."

The Teaching of the Bible

An unplanned abortion or a miscarriage can result at any time, because of our human imperfection, or from something like a car accident. However, an operation or other intervention to end a pregnancy by removing an embryo or fetus from the womb is a different matter. According to the God's Word, as the above has demonstrated, abortion is willfully taking a human life, for which God will expect a life for that life. It is not an unforgivable sin if you have already had an abortion, before coming to an accurate knowledge of the Scriptures, but you must repent from that sin, and turn around, never doing it again.

Romans 14:12 English Standard Version (ESV)

¹² So then each of us will give an account of himself to God.

Scarred Emotionally for Life

Some may believe that abortion is an easy resolution to an unexpected pregnancy. However, abortion can very much make life far more difficult ti live. Some Bible writers revealed to their readers that there is an ongoing conflict within the Christian, with one side being the fallen, sinful flesh. In this revelation, the Bible writers use such expressions as "the inner man," "our inner man," and comparable expressions. At Romans 2:14-15, Paul speaks of us saying, "The law is written on their hearts." Because man and woman were made in the image and likeness of God, they were given a **moral nature** that was in harmony with God. This moral nature produces a mental power or ability such as reason and conscience. Even though, we are imperfect, we retain a measure of this moral nature that is in harmony with God's moral standards. This moral nature operates in "the inner man," as a law, a **moral law**. However, because of our fallen condition, there is also 'the **law of sin**, which is in our members.' This 'law in our members of our body, wages a war against the law of our mind and can make us a prisoner of the law of sin.' (Rom. 6:12; 7:22, 23) Abortion would violate our moral nature of right and wrong, the measure of conscience that God had originally given Adam and Eve. Moreover, abortion would demand that a young woman close her tender heart and compassions to the tiny life growing within her. (See 1 John 3:17) How disheartening!

What may not be appreciated are the emotions that come after the abortion. There will be this unrelenting feeling of guilt and shame at taking another human life. Even a police officer that shoots a wicked criminal in the line of duty is obligated by the department to seek out counseling, to deal with the taking of a life. Imagine how much more so this will be with a mother, who takes the life of her unborn baby. This emotional trauma will never go away. When the due date of the bay comes, it will be emotional losses, which you have never known, and it will be revisited upon you every birthday, every holiday that child would never enjoy with you.

Get the Help and Care

Almost everyone has family or friends of some sort, who will help you during and after the pregnancy. They can provide emotional, physical, mental, spiritual, and financial assistance. Most countries have some kind of assistance for mothers as well. Many years down the road, when you look back on this decision, it will be just the opposite of the pain you would have suffered, nothing but peace of heart and mind, as you look at your young child.

BASIC TEACHING: Does the Bible Teach Universal Salvation?

Universal Salvation, Christian Universalism, or simply Universalism) is the doctrine that all sinful persons, who are alienated from God, because of God's great divine love and mercy, will eventually be reconciled to God. Bible Scholar Richard Bauckham outlines the history of universal salvation,

> The history of the doctrine of universal salvation (or *apokatastasis*) is a remarkable one. Until the nineteenth century, almost all Christian theologians taught the reality of eternal torment in hell. Here and there, outside the theological mainstream, were some who believed that the wicked would be finally annihilated (in its commonest form, this is the doctrine of 'conditional immortality').[22] Even fewer were the advocates of universal salvation, though these few included some major theologians of the early church. Eternal punishment was firmly asserted in

---

[22] For details see L. E. Froom, *The Conditionalist Faith of Our Fathers* (Washington, DC: Review and Herald, 1965–1966).

official creeds and confessions of the churches. It must have seemed as indispensable a part of universal Christian belief as the doctrines of the Trinity and the incarnation. Since 1800 this situation has entirely changed, and no traditional Christian doctrine has been so widely abandoned as that of eternal punishment. Its advocates among theologians today must be fewer than ever before. The alternative interpretation of hell as annihilation seems to have prevailed even among many of the more conservative theologians. Among the less conservative, universal salvation, either as hope or as dogma, is now so widely accepted that many theologians assume it virtually without argument.[23]

"Modern Universalists claim that this doctrine is contained in the New Testament in the teachings of Jesus, and conforms to the laws of nature as taught by science and sanctioned by reason and philosophy."[24] One reason behind the Universalist mindset is, there dislike

---

[23] Richard Bauckham, "Universalism: a historical survey", Themelios 4.2 (September 1978): 47–54.
[24] Microsoft ® Encarta ® 2006. © 1993-2005 Microsoft Corporation. All rights reserved.

of the hellfire doctrine,[25] where the sinner is punished, i.e., tormented for an eternity. For the Universalist, eternal torment for one, who is born imperfect, with a natural desire toward sin, which Genesis argues is mentally bent toward wickedness, and has a heart, which is treacherous and unknowable, would be a sign of injustice, and an unloving God.

The Salvation Debate

1 Corinthians 15:25, 28 English Standard Version (ESV)

[25] For he must reign until he has put all his enemies under his feet. [28] When all things are subjected to him, then the Son himself will also be subjected to him who put all things in subjection under him, that God may **be all in all**.

The Good News Translations renders that last clause and prepositional phrase, "God will rule completely over all." The Universalist would say that if God were going to "be all in all or if "God will rule completely over all" he would need to reconcile **all** humans to himself

---

[25] Please see Volume 1 of this series, *Basic Teachings of the Bible*, article titled, Is Hell a Place of eternal Torment.

eventually. Another text often used by the Universalist.

Philippians 2:10-11 Updated American Standard Version (UASV)

¹⁰ so that at the name of Jesus **every knee should bow**, of those who are in heaven and on earth and under the earth, ¹¹ and **every tongue confess** that Jesus Christ is Lord, to the glory of God the Father.

Here the Universalist would argue that if "**every** knee should to bow" "and **every** tongue confess," it must follow that every human that has lived up unto the time of Christ's return will be reconciled to God in the end.

They would also point to,

Romans 5:18 English Standard Version (ESV)

¹⁸ Therefore, as one trespass led to condemnation for all men, so one act of righteousness leads to justification and life **for all men**.

"One trespass"–"One act of righteousness"

"Condemnation"–"Justification"

"All men [in Adam]"–"All men [in Christ]"

It would seem at first that this text is a perfect balance, in that Adam's one sinful act contributed to **all** of humanity inheriting sin and imperfection, and Christ one act as a ransom sacrifice would contribute to **all** of humanity receiving life. Before delving into a response for these verses, let us see what the Bible teaches. First, though, just know that, when you have a few Scriptures that appear to be in opposition to many Scriptures, you likely do not understand the few correctly.

The Bible Teaches

The Scriptures, which make all too clear that some will not be receiving salvation, are so abundant from Genesis to Revelation. Adam committed the most egregious sin of any human alive, as he, in essence, murdered billions of humans, by his rebellion. For this reason, Adam was told, "for you are dust, and to dust you shall return." (Gen. 3:19) Revelation 21:8 says, "But as for the cowardly, the faithless, the detestable, as for murderers, the sexually immoral, sorcerers, idolaters, and all liars, their portion will be in the lake that burns with fire and sulfur, which is the second death." There is not one verse in the Bible that speaks of redemption or a resurrection from "the second death."

Matthew 25:46 English Standard Version (ESV)

⁴⁶ And these [unrighteous] will go away into **eternal punishment** [*Kolasin*, lopping off, cutting off], but the righteous into eternal life."

Kolasin "akin to *kolazoo*"[26] "This means 'to cut short,' 'to lop,' 'to trim,' and figuratively a. 'to impede,' 'restrain,' and b. 'to punish,' and in the passive 'to suffer loss.'[27] The first part of the sentence is only in harmony with the second part of the sentence, if the eternal punishment is eternal death. The wicked receive eternal death and the righteous eternal life. We might note that Matthews Gospel was primarily for the Jewish Christians, and under the Mosaic Law, God would punish those who violated the law, saying they "shall be cut off [penalty of death] from Israel." (Ex 12:15; Lev 20:2-3) We need further to consider,

---

[26] W. E. Vine, Merrill F. Unger, and William White Jr., *Vine's Complete Expository Dictionary of Old and New Testament Words* (Nashville, TN: T. Nelson, 1996), 498.

[27] Gerhard Kittel, Gerhard Friedrich, and Geoffrey William Bromiley, *Theological Dictionary of the New Testament* (Grand Rapids, MI: W.B. Eerdmans, 1985), 451.

2 Thessalonians 1:8-9 English Standard Version (ESV)

⁸ in flaming fire, inflicting vengeance on those who do not know God and on those who do not obey the gospel of our Lord Jesus. ⁹ They will suffer the punishment of **eternal destruction**, away from the presence of the Lord and from the glory of his might

Notice that Paul says, the punishment for the wicked is "eternal destruction." Many times in talking with those that support the position of eternal torment in some hellfire, they will add a word to Matthew 25:46 in their paraphrase of the verse, '*conscious* eternal punishment.' However, Jesus does not tell us what the eternal punishment is, just that it is a punishment and it is eternal. Therefore, those who support eternal conscious fiery torment will read the verse to mean just that, while those, who hold to the position of eternal destruction, will take Matthew 25:46 to mean that. Considering that Jesus does not define what the eternal punishment is, this verse is not a proof text for either side of the hellfire argument.

Hebrews 2:14 English Standard Version (ESV)

14 Since therefore the children share in flesh and blood, he himself likewise partook of the same things, that through death he might **destroy the one** who has the power of death, that is, the devil,

Yes, Jesus' ransom sacrifice will cause the destruction of Satan the Devil. The unrighteous, also known as the wicked within the Bible are "vessels of wrath prepared for **destruction**." (Rom 9:22) Yes, "the years of the wicked are cut short." (Pro 10:27) According to Vine's Expository Dictionary of Old and New Testament Words, *olothreuo* means "'to destroy,' especially in the sense of slaying, while "*katargeo*" means, "to reduce to inactivity." In addition, *apollumi* signifies "to destroy utterly."

The Universalist likes to stress one quality of God, taking it beyond its balanced limits, that is *mercy*. However, they ignore the other quality that mercy is balanced with, namely *justice*. God had clearly told Adam, "of the tree of the knowledge of good and evil you shall not eat, for in the day that you eat of it you shall surely die." (Gen. 2:17) The apostle Paul tells us, "The wages of sin is death." (Rom. 6:23) The prophet Ezekiel recorded God as saying, "the soul [person] who sins shall die." (Eze. 18:4, 20) God is selective in his mercy/justice, as he said, "I will be gracious to whom I will be gracious, and will show mercy on whom I will show mercy." (Ex 33:19) God has provide the ransom sacrifice of his Son (Matt 20:28), to cover over Adamic sin, not the willful unrepentant practicing of sin. (Heb. 6:4; 10:26; 2 Pet 2:21)

Where did the Universalist go wrong? As they overplayed the *mercy*, while downplaying *justice*, they also overemphasize the God of love. (1 John 4:8) They are unable to wrap their mind around the God of love, who also possess the quality of justice, and even seeks vengeance on behalf of the righteous, which were treated wickedly.

However, it is also the **un**biblical doctrine of hellfire and eternal torment, which moved them emotionally into another **un**biblical doctrine, universal salvation. They would have been wiser to set aside the eternal torment in a burning hell as being **un**biblical; recognizing that punishment for one's actions that fit the offense is biblical. The position of the Annihilationist is that of eternal destruction as a punishment, which does not involve an eternal conscious torment, as it would not be compatible with the God of love, nor his justice.[28]

Exodus 21:24 English Standard Version (ESV)

[24] eye for eye, tooth for tooth, hand for hand, foot for foot,

Another possibility as to why they hold to the position of universal salvation is the other **un**biblical doctrine of immortality of all souls. This belief is that once God created a human being, bring him or her into existence, they must live forever in some fashion (physical or spiritual body), and in some place (earth, heaven, or hell). Since the Universalist arrived at the correct conclusion that God would not torture an imperfect human, who sinned for 70-80 years, by burning him forever, they just removed the place of hell (wrongly thought of as a place of eternal torment) from the equation, and accepted that all would eventually be reconciled to God. They could have simply looked at the original language words, and rightly concluded that the Hebrew *sheol* and Greek *hades* are not places of eternal torment, but rather the gravedom of mankind, with the punishment being eternal death.

---

[28] http://bible-translation.net/page/is-hell-a-place-of-eternal-torment

"*Athanasia* lit., "deathlessness" (*a*, negative, *thanatos*, "death"), is rendered "immortality" in 1 Cor. 15:53, 54, of the glorified body of the believer." (Vine 1996, Volume 2, Page 321) There are no verses within the Bible, which says that every human has an inherent quality of immortality. Rather, as we have already seen, Adam was sentenced to death for rebelling against God, as well as God himself saying by way of his authors, "The soul that sins shall die" and "the wages of sin is death."

Romans 6:23 English Standard Version (ESV)

²³ For the wages of sin is death, but the free gift of God is eternal life in Christ Jesus our Lord.

If every human were created with absolute eternal life within him or her; then, there would be no gift for God to give. God has given humanity free will and the right to choose. He said to the Israelites, who wanted to be his people, "I call heaven and earth to witness against you today, that I have set before you life and death, blessing and curse. Therefore choose life, that you and your offspring may live" (Deut. 30:19) In other words, man can choose to live by the righteous laws of his Creator, or he can choose to lose his life in a rebellion against his Creator. God's justice does not allow him to have wicked persons living forever among the righteous. Adam and Eve did not fully appreciate what God had done for them, such as the eternal life he set before them, a paradise garden that they were to grow until it encompassed the entire earth, and filling the earth with perfect descendants; therefore, they returned to the dust that they came from. The same exact choice is before each of us.

What about Philippians 2:10-11, "so that at the name of Jesus **every knee should bow**, of those who are in heaven and on earth and under the earth, and **every tongue confess** that Jesus Christ is Lord, to the glory of God the Father." A day is coming when all of the wicked will receive their punishment of everlasting destruction. Therefore, all who are alive on earth and in heaven will be submitting themselves to the sovereignty of God. Then, the verse will hold true, 'every knee will bow,' 'and every tongue will confess that Jesus Christ is Lord.' Thus, the knees and the tongues of the unrighteous, rebellious ones will no longer be in existence, as they will have been destroyed.

What about the argument of Romans 5:18 that Adam's one sinful act contributed to **all** of humanity inheriting sin and imperfection, and

Christ one act as a ransom sacrifice would contribute to **all** of humanity receiving life. As was stated earlier, when you have a couple verses that seem to be in conflict with many verses from Genesis to Revelation, it means that you are likely misunderstanding the couple of verses. The Scripters clearly show that only the righteous receive life. Adam was not forced to received eternal life; it was a gift from God, which was based upon his remaining faithful. Therefore, when he rejected that gift and was unfaithful, the gift of life was taken away. Thus, the same would hold true for Adam's descendants as well.–Ezekiel 18:31-32

As you will see, "all" in Greek does not necessarily mean "all." The Greek word behind "all" is *pan*, which comes in various forms. 1 John 2:2 says that Jesus is a covering "for the sins of the **whole world**."[29] Paul says at 1 Timothy 2:6 that Jesus "gave himself as a ransom for **all** [*pantōn*, all (ones)]." Romans 5:18 says, 'Christ's one act as a ransom sacrifice would contribute to **all** [*pantas*] of humanity receiving life.' Titus 2:10 says, "For the grace of God has appeared, bringing salvation to **all** [*pasin*] men." While this seems quite clear on

---

[29] This verses is included because it convey the same message, but it does not contain the Greek *pan*. Rather, it has *holos*, meaning "whole, complete, entirely."

the surface, it is not really so. What do we do with the other verses that say only redeemable humankind will receive salvation, that is, those that repent and turnaround from their former course. (Acts 17:30, John 3:16, 1 Jn. 5:12)

Yes, not **all** is so black and white, once the interpreter looks beneath the surface. Many times the Greek word (*panta*) rendered "all" is often used in a hyperbolic sense. For example, at Luke 21:29, in speaking of a parable, it is said, "Look at the fig tree (*suke*), and **all** the trees. (*panta ta dendra*)" While the literal translation seems nonsensical, this is what pushes the reader to look deeper. The Good News Translation gives us the meaning in "Think of the fig tree and all the other trees." "Other" is not in the Greek, but English translations add words to complete the sense in the English. Regardless, the "all" in many verses, including these, is being used hyperbolically.

At Acts 2:17, Peter at Pentecost speaks of the prophecy in the Old Testament book of Joel, saying, "And in the last days it shall be, God declares, that I will pour out my Spirit on **all** [*pasan*] flesh." Was the Spirit poured out literally on **all** flesh at Pentecost? No, it was only 120 initially, and eventually a few thousand, out of millions then alive. Repeatedly when the term "all" is used in the Greek New

Testament, "all" is not literally meant as "all," but rather hyperbolically to emphasize. It can have the sense of "all others," "all sorts, "all kinds," and so on. Keep in mind that God did pour his Spirit out on 'sons and daughters, young men and old men, even on my male slaves and on my female slaves.'

Another example would be at Luke 11:42, which reads, "But woe to you Pharisees! For you tithe mint and rue and every [*pan*] herb, and neglect justice and the love of God." It should be noted that both the mint and the rue are herbs. Thus, the GNT[30] renders it, "all the **other** herbs." While this author accepts the literal translations as being closest to the Word of God in English,[31] they can infer that that the mint and rue are not herbs, while the dynamic equivalent translations clear it up.

Unbiblical Teaching

The universal salvation position that **all** humans will eventually be reconciled to God, receiving salvation, is unbiblical. God has given humanity free will, and as free moral persons,

---

[30] Good News Translation (GNT)

[31] The literal translations are the best for both Bible reading and personal Bible study, and the ambiguity of this text would be cleared up for those who research.

they have the ability to reject his sovereignty. Moreover, if universal salvation were true, it would be at odds with the very reason God allowed humanity to go on after the sin of Adam, as opposed to just starting over. Satan had challenged the sovereignty of God and the integrity of humans, saying that they would not remain faithful to God, if they faced adversity. If all, were to be saved anyway (including Satan), why would God have bothered to direct Satan's attention to the integrity of Job, pointing out that humans can choose to be faithful in adverse times?

Universal salvation is a feel-good **un**biblical doctrine that our imperfect flesh wants to be true, and Satan wants us to accept as true. It allows us to not be concerned about our actions or deeds, as one will receive salvation regardless. What they are doing is removing integrity and faithfulness from the equation. However, Like Adam, who betrayed God, Like Judas Iscariot, who betrayed the Son of God, and all the rest, who have rejected God,

Hebrews 6:4-6 English Standard Version (ESV)

⁴ For it is impossible, in the case of those who have once been enlightened, who have tasted the heavenly gift, and have shared in the

Holy Spirit,[5] and have tasted the goodness of the word of God and the powers of the age to come,[6] and then have fallen away, to restore them again to repentance, since they are crucifying once again the Son of God to their own harm and holding him up to contempt.

Jesus, in speaking to the Father about his disciples, said,

John 17:12 English Standard Version (ESV)

[12] While I was with them, I kept them in your name, which you have given me. I have guarded them, and not one of them has been lost except the son of destruction, that the Scripture might be fulfilled.

The apostle Paul made it all too clear, as to the outcome of willful unrepentant sinners,

Hebrews 10:26-31 English Standard Version (ESV)

[26] For if we go on sinning deliberately after receiving the knowledge of the truth, there no longer remains a sacrifice for sins, [27] but a fearful expectation of judgment, and a fury of fire that will consume the adversaries. [28] Anyone who has set aside the law of Moses dies without mercy on the evidence of two or three witnesses. [29] How much worse punishment, do you think, will be

deserved by the one who has trampled underfoot the Son of God, and has profaned the blood of the covenant by which he was sanctified, and has outraged the Spirit of grace? ³⁰ For we know him who said, "Vengeance is mine; I will repay." And again, "The Lord will judge his people." ³¹ It is a fearful thing to fall into the hands of the living God.

There have been many goodhearted self-declared Christians from the second to the twenty-first century, who have held to the **un**biblical position of universal salvation. Again, this is not a biblical teaching. While it is true that "God is love" (1 John 4:8), it is just as true that he is a God of "justice" (Isa. 33:22; Ps 33:5; Job 37:23) As a God of love, he gives us free moral agents the choice between life and death, if we choose to live under his sovereignty, we receive eternal life. As a God of Justice, if we choose to reject his sovereignty, he rejects us, and we receive eternal destruction.

BASIC TEACHING: What Is Inerrancy of Scripture?

As you may know, there are several different levels of inerrancy. **Absolute Inerrancy** is the belief that the Bible is fully true and exact in every way; including not only relationships and doctrine, but also science and history. In other words, all information is completely exact. **Full Inerrancy** is the belief that the Bible was not written as a science or historical textbook, but is phenomenological, in that it is written from the human perspective. In other words, speaking of such things as the sun rising (still used today), the four corners of the earth (still used today), or the rounding off number approximations are all from a human perspective. **Limited Inerrancy** is the belief that the Bible is meant only as a reflection of God's purposes and will, so the science and history is the understanding of the author's day, and is limited. Thus, the Bible is susceptible to errors in these areas. **Inerrancy of Purpose** is the belief that it is only inerrant in the purpose of bringing its readers to a saving faith. The Bible is not about facts, but about persons and relationships, thus, it is subject to error. Inspired: Not Inerrant is the belief that its authors are human and thus subject to human error. It should be noted that **this author holds the position of <u>full inerrancy</u>**.

For many today, the Bible is nothing more than a book written by men, which is full of myths and legends, contradictions, as well as geographical, historical, and scientific errors. University professor Gerald A. Larue had this to say, "The views of the writers as expressed in the Bible reflect the ideas, beliefs, and concepts current in their own times and are limited by the extent of knowledge in those times." (Larue 1983, 39) On the other hand, the Bible's claims are quite different.

2 Timothy 3:16, 17 (HCSB): *All Scripture is inspired by God* and is profitable for teaching, for rebuking, for correcting, for training in righteousness, so that the man of God may be complete, equipped for every good work.

2 Peter 1:21 (ESV): For no prophecy was ever produced by the will of man, but men spoke from God as they were carried along by the Holy Spirit.

Below are two very good examples from the 20th century history of Inerrancy of Scripture, and the pattern of behavior, which has now become the norm. Both examples are from *Defending Inerrancy: Affirming the*

Accuracy of Scripture for a New Generation, by Geisler, Norman L.; Roach, Bill (2012).

EXAMPLE ONE

The rift over inerrancy remained simmering on the back burner. Two important factors gave impetus to the limited inerrancy movement (that inerrancy was limited to only redemptive matters). First, neoevangelicalism arose originally from a sermon by Ockenga in 1948 at the Civic Auditorium in Pasadena. It was a call to repudiate separationism and involve evangelicals in social action while retaining a commitment to fundamental doctrines like inerrancy. It was not initially designed as a movement, but the name caught on as it was used by Edward Carnell and Harold Lindsell, and also by Carl Henry (who had already written The Uneasy Conscience of Modern Fundamentalism, 1947); Gleason Archer also began to support it. Soon after this, younger evangelicals started to join the movement, and the doctrinal emphasis was downplayed until inerrancy was no longer a characteristic of the group.

EXAMPLE TWO

According to Harold Lindsell (Battle for the Bible, chap. 6), in 1947 Charles Fuller invited Ockenga to join him in founding a School of Missions and Evangelism. "Biblical inerrancy" was part of the doctrinal statement. Harold Lindsell was the first dean and with Wilbur Smith, Everett F. Harrison, and Carl Henry formed the first faculty. The doctrinal statement of Scripture read: "The books which form the canon of the Old and New Testaments as originally given are plenarily inspired and free from all error in the whole and in the part. These books constitute the written Word of God, the only infallible rule of faith and practice." Such a statement meant that the Bible is free from errors in matters of fact, science, history, and chronology, as well as in matters having to do with salvation.

Within the ensuing years, doubts began to arise on the Fuller board and faculty about the inerrancy of Scripture. First, Fuller staff member Bela Vassady said his honesty kept him from signing the inerrancy part of the doctrinal

128

statement, and he voluntarily left the school. By 1962 it became apparent that others at Fuller no longer believed in inerrancy. One wealthy and influential board member, C. David Weyerhaeuser, came to the conviction that the Bible was not inerrant. Two other faculty members came to the same conclusion, but neither was asked to leave the school. The founder's son, Daniel Fuller (after studying under Karl Barth in Basel), soon followed suit. Calvin Schoonhoven admitted that he did not believe in inerrancy when he was hired. Finally, David Hubbard was hired as president in spite of the fact that the syllabus on the Old Testament he had coauthored with Robert Laurin stated that Adam was not historical, Moses had not written the whole Pentateuch, and Daniel was written after the great world kingdom events that are recorded as prophecies in his book (though Hubbard maintained that his own views were orthodox).

In December 1962, "Black Saturday" occurred at a faculty-trustee meeting in Pasadena. Here a number of faculty and board members expressed that they did not believe in the inerrancy of Scripture. Edward Johnson declared his belief that inerrancy was a "benchmark" belief and resigned because the board failed to take its stand on inerrancy (which was still in the doctrinal statement from its beginning).

Geisler goes through numerous situations like the above, where good men, with great intentions for a group or school that accepts full or total inerrancy, and over time, member after member begins to abandon the whole purpose of founding the group or school. In the end, the group or school is not different from the state or liberal run groups and institutions. It seems that "conservative," "fundamental," Christians are scared to walk the path alone, being few in number, so they cower to those, who have abandoned the faith, believing we can associate ourselves with those who have abandoned the faith. What Would Jesus, Peter, Paul, James, or John say?

Acts 20:27-30 English Standard Version (ESV)

[27] for I did not shrink from declaring to you the whole counsel of God. [28] Pay careful attention to yourselves and to all the flock, in

which the Holy Spirit has made you overseers, to care for the church of God, which he obtained with his own blood. ²⁹ I know that after my departure fierce wolves will come in among you, not sparing the flock; ³⁰ and **from among your own selves will arise men speaking twisted things**, to draw away **the** disciples after them.

The opposition to the Truth and the Way did not come without numerous warnings from Jesus and the New Testament writers. Beginning with Jesus, the warning went out.

"[Jesus] Be Aware of False Prophets . . .

[Peter] There Will Be False Teachers Among You"

Jesus was well aware that the easiest way to defeat any group is to divide them, and so was Satan, who had been watching humanity for over 4,000 years, and especially the Israelites (Isaac and Ishmael / Jacob and Esau / Israel and Judah), as "Satan disguises himself as an angel of light. So it is no surprise if his servants, also, disguise themselves as servants of righteousness." (2 Cor. 11:14-15)

Where would these false teachers come from? Paul clearly says, to the Ephesian elders, about 56 C.E., "**from among your own selves** will arise men speaking twisted things." (Ac 20:29-30) Yes, these ones, who stand off from the Truth and the Way, would not be seeking their own disciples, but rather they would be seeking, "to draw away the disciples after them." i.e., the disciples of Christ.

The apostle Peter also spoke of these things about 64 C.E., "there will be false teachers among you, who will secretly bring in destructive heresies . . . in their greed they will exploit you with false words.." (2 Pet. 2:1, 3) These ones abandon the faithful words, become false teachers, rising within the Christian congregation, sharing their corrupting influence, intending to hide, disguise, or mislead.

These dire warnings by Jesus and the New Testament Authors had their beginnings in the first century C.E. Yes, they began small, but burst forth on the scene in the second century.

"[Paul says it] Is Already at Work"

About 51 C.E., some 18-years after Jesus' death, resurrection and ascension, division was already starting to creep into the faith, "the mystery of lawlessness is already at work." (2 Thess. 2:7) Yes, the power of the **lawlessness** was already present, which is the power of Satan, the god of this world (2 Cor. 4:4), and his tens of millions of demons, are hard at work behind the scenes.

There was even some divisions beginning as early as 49 C.E., when the elders wrote a letter to the Gentile believers, saying, "Since we have heard that some persons have gone out from us and troubled you with words, unsettling your minds, although we gave them no instructions" (Ac 15:24) Here we see that some *within*, were being very vocal about their opposition to the direction the faith was heading. Here, it was over whether the Gentiles needed to be circumcised, to be obedient to the Mosaic Law. (Ac 15:1, 5)

As the years progressed throughout the first-century, this divisive "talk ... spread like gangrene." (2 Tim. 2:17, c 65 C.E.) About 51 C.E., They had some in Thessalonica, at worst, going ahead of, or at best, misunderstanding Paul, and wrongly stating by word and a bogus letter "that the day of the Lord has come." (2 Thess. 2:1-2) In Corinth, about 55 C.E., "some of [were saying] that there is no resurrection of the dead. (1 Cor. 15:12) About 65 C.E., some were "saying that the resurrection has already happened. They [were] upsetting the faith of some." (2 Tim 2:16-18)

Throughout the next three decades, no inspired books were written. However, by the time of the apostle John's letter writing days of 96-98 C.E., he tells us, "Now many antichrists have come. Therefore we know that it is the last hour." (1 John 2:18) These are ones, "who denies that Jesus is the Christ" and ones who not confess "Jesus Christ has come in the flesh is from God." (1 John 2:22; 4:2-3)

From 33 C.E. to 100 C.E., the apostles served Christ as a restraint against the great apostasy that was coming. Paul stated at 2 Thessalonians 2:7, "For the mystery of lawlessness is already at work. Only he [Apostle by Christ] who now restrains it [the great apostasy] will do so until he **[apostles]** is out of the way." 2 Thessalonians 2:3 said, "Let no one deceive you in any way **[misinterpretation or false teachers of Paul's first letter]**. For that day **[presence (second coming) of Christ]** will not come, unless the rebellion **[apostasy]** comes first, and the man of lawlessness **[likely one person, or maybe an organization/movement, empowered by Satan]** is revealed, the son of destruction"

We must keep in mind that the meaning of any given text is what the author meant by the words that he used, as should have been understood by his audience, and had some relevance/meaning for his audience. The rebellion [apostasy] began slowly in the first century, and would break forth after the death of the last apostle. Historians Will and Ariel Durant state, "Celsus [second-century enemy of Christianity] himself had sarcastically observed that Christians were 'split up into ever so many factions, each individual desiring to have his own party.' About 187 [C.E.] Irenaeus listed twenty varieties of Christianity; about 384 [C.E.] Epiphanius counted eighty." (*The Story of Civilization: Part III—Caesar and Christ*) Today we have 41,000 varieties of Christianity. What does it mean for the Christian, who has not abandoned inerrancy of Scripture, when someone abandons full or total inerrancy of Scripture? Let us listen to the words of Dr. Wayne Grudem,

> Some theologians have argued that since human language is always in some sense "imperfect," any message that God addresses to us in human language must also be limited in its authority or truthfulness. But these passages and many others that record instances of God's words of personal address to individuals give no indication of any limitation of the authority or

truthfulness of God's words when they are spoken in human language. Quite the contrary is true, for the words always place an absolute obligation upon the hearers to believe them and to obey them fully. **To disbelieve or disobey any part of them is to disbelieve or disobey God himself.** (Bold mine) Grudem, Wayne (2011). Making Sense of the Bible: One of Seven Parts from Grudem's Systematic Theology (Making Sense of Series) (p. 35). Zondervan.

The Foundational Doctrine

Inerrancy of Scripture has to be the foundational doctrine, like no other. Why? If you remove it, you have no other. If inerrancy of Scripture is true, and it is, and one was teaching that it is not, what does that make them? If you willfully teach something that is not true, but rather is false, even though you believe it to be true, does that not make you a false teacher? A prophet of God is also and primarily so, a proclaimer of God's Word, namely, a teacher. What happens to false prophets and false teachers? God will deal with them his way, at Jesus' return, but for now, they are to be expelled from the church. What did John say, as to how we were to treat these ones? Did he say that we were to socialize with them, but just disagree with them doctrinally?

2 John 1:9-11 English Standard Version (ESV)

⁹ Everyone who goes on ahead and does not abide in the teaching of Christ, does not have God. Whoever abides in the teaching has both the Father and the Son. ¹⁰ If anyone comes to you and does not bring this teaching, do not receive him into your house or give him any greeting, ¹¹ for whoever greets him takes part in his wicked works.

"The teaching of Christ may refer to the teachings of Jesus or to teachings about Jesus. In either case, it refers to orthodox truth established and accepted in the church." The Holman New Testament Commentary by David Walls and Max Anders (p. 240) Yes, false teachers introduce their corrupt thinking into the church, and so should be removed to preserve the spirit of the church. Once removed, if unrepentant, what does John say our attitude toward them should be? We all have heard the phrase, 'guilt by association,' which means that when we socialize beyond being cordial; we are just as guilty as they are in the eyes of God. If a man wearing a clean white glove shakes the hand of a man wearing a soil-covered glove, does the clean clove make the dirty glove cleaner? On the other hand, does the grimy glove, make the clean glove dirtier?

These verses [1 John 1:9-11] seem harsh. Those who remain faithful to the teaching of Christ must resist those who do not. If a person did not teach truth about Jesus, these believers were not to practice hospitality toward him. This does not suggest that we are not to be cordial to false teachers, or that we cannot invite a member of a false sect into our home to talk with him. Rather, it refers to a level of hospitality that helps the false teacher spread his or her false doctrine.

In the first century, traveling was difficult. The traveler could not find hotels and restaurants. Traveling teachers and missionaries depended on others to house and feed them. John urged his readers not to "fund" these false teachers by housing and feeding them. To do so would be to share **in his wicked work.** In our day, when people of all sorts of religious belief use the media to plead for financial support, we need to be careful what kind of doctrine we fund. (IBID, 241)

The irony here is when authors like David Walls and Max Anders pen their commentaries, they are likely thinking of Jehovah's Witnesses, Mormons, and others as being the false teachers, by means of referring to them as a "false sect." Really? Is the rejection of the Trinity by the Jehovah's Witnesses any worse than the so-called Christian (Baptist, Presbyterian, etc.), who rejects the very Word of God that expounds on that doctrine and every other doctrine that is held dear? When someone is an unrepentant false teacher, they are to be removed from the church, and are not to be invited to social gatherings, nor are they to be spoken of in flattering terms within spoken or written words. If they repent, turn around, and change their ways, then time must pass, to see if this is really the case. Anyone standing off from the truth is an apostate of the church, an enemy of the church.

BASIC TEACHING: Does the Bible Teach Liberation Theology?

Socioeconomic Criticism is yet one more form of biblical criticism that has emerged in recent years, referring to features of ancient social life expressed in the biblical texts and to rebuild the social worlds behind the texts. In and of itself, historical criticism from its inception has shown an interest the social side of things, as it has covered nations, states, social groups, as well as religious movements. Nevertheless, in the 1960s and early 1970s social-scientific investigation came into a specialized field of study.

> Liberation hermeneutics is the interpretation of biblical and related texts from a self-conscious perspective and program of social transformation. It is practiced in any number of ways, depending on how the situation of oppression and the agenda of liberation are formulated and addressed. (McKenzie and Hayes 1999, 283)

For decades now, many of the Third World countries in Africa, Asia, and Latin America are disadvantaged in the extreme and mired in innumerable ways. The people who were and are so unfortunate to have been born in these countries lay the blame at the feet of their governments or local religious leaders, accusing them of oppression. Others still, hold that it is foreign debt that lies at the root of the problem. However, in the 1960 and early 1970s, there arose what some thought would solve what was known as a Third World[32] problem, liberation theology.

Protestant and Catholic theologians met in Sri Lanka in 1981, at the First Ecumenical Assembly of Third World Theologians. The Second Ecumenical Assembly of Third World Theologians was held on December 8, 1986, with more than 2,000 persons, mostly Catholics, who met at Mexico City's National Autonomous University of Mexico (UNAM) to discuss "Liberation Theology in the Third World." What was the resolve behind these assemblies? They wanted to know what progress had been made within liberation

---

[32] Third World lands are less developed nations: the developing nations of Africa, Asia, and Latin America, generally less economically advanced than the industrialized nations but with varied economies. Originally the Third World was contrasted with the First World, the capitalist industrial nations, and the Second World, the industrialized Communist nations.

theology, and what the future looked like for the movement.

Our question almost thirty years later is, 'how has liberation theology affected the Third World?' Has it achieved its objectives? Is it the way of the future? We can best address those questions by first investigating what liberation theology is and what it had envisioned to bring about.

Liberation Theology

According to Brazilian Catholic theologian Frei Betto says that liberation theology is a "critical reflection on the practice of liberating the poor, having as basis the Bible, Christian tradition, and the teachings of the ecclesiastical magisterium." Webster's Dictionary says liberation theology is "a religious movement especially among Roman Catholic clergy in Latin America that combines political philosophy usually of a Marxist orientation with a theology of salvation as liberation from injustice."[33] However, what system is considered essential for this "practice" of liberation?

---

[33] Inc Merriam-Webster, Merriam-Webster's Collegiate Dictionary., Eleventh ed. (Springfield, MA: Merriam-Webster, Inc., 2003).

Liberation theologians have held that the use of force and physical violence is perfectly acceptable in some counties. Therefore, revolutions against the government, such as those of the late 1970s and the 1980s in Nicaragua and the Philippines, are not only accepted by liberation-theology followers but urged on. The result is their being fully involved in politics. Frei Betto made the claim that "it is impossible to live our faith in isolation from politics." Really? What is the evidence for such a position?

These liberation theologians assert that the Bible is their source of "inspiration" as a backing for liberation theology. Peruvian liberation theologian Gustavo Gutiérrez, who is viewed as the "father of liberation theology," argues, "The liberation of Israel is a political action. It is the breaking away from a situation of despoliation and misery and the beginning of despoliation and misery and the beginning of the construction of a just a fraternal society." (Gutierrez 1988, 161)

However, far more significant to liberation theologians is what they label "Christian Base communities." within the community over submission to church authority and, as their very name suggests, made power seem to flow from the bottom or base upward. With the guidance of liberation theology, the conversations within the church were concerned with the material circumstances and concerns over class interests. A Base Christian community is a small group who came together to study the Bible, and then act consistent with social justice focused on Christianity, this being especially common among the third world and the poor. Within these small groups of mostly persons that could barely read or write, if at all, you had the pastors offering them a level of education, but also calling them to political action. Within Brazil of the 1980s, there were more than four million Catholics, who were members of some 70,000 of these Christian Base communities.

Liberation Theology and the Pope

On August 6, 1984, the Pope issued Instruction on Some Aspects of Liberation Theology, accusing it of being "a perversion of the Christian message." The Vatican stated, "Systematically or deliberately resorting to blind violence, from wherever it may come, should be condemned."

The following year the Vatican made it position known by taking action against the utmost provocative liberation theologian,

Brazilian Franciscan priest Leonardo Boff, punishing with one year of "penitential silence." However, shortly thereafter, change was coming.

Boff was not only given amnesty, but Rome changed its tone in the new release of the Instruction on Christian Freedom and Liberation, which said that it is "fully legitimate that those who suffer oppression from the holders of wealth or of political power should act with morally licit means, in order to obtain the structures and institutions in which their rights may be truly respected." In other words, it was not believed to be acceptable to take up arms. Pope John Paul II thereafter sent a letter to the Brazilian bishops, which said, "Liberation Theology is not only opportune but also useful and necessary for Latin America." What brought about this new outlook? The Catholic Church said therein that they were helping the people "to respond to the anxiety of contemporary man as he endures oppression and yearns for freedom."

Looking back, one might be more inclined to see it as more of a case of great pressure within the Catholic Church that brought about this about face on liberation theology. After Boff received his penalty, two cardinals and four bishops descended on Rome, to defend his liberation theology. Another ten bishops signed off on a letter that viewed his penalty a setback to human rights. Moreover, there were Catholic priests all over the Third World wrapped up in liberation work.

The Church Set Against the Theologians

Clearly, the Catholic Church, opposed with contentious persons within its ranks, was attempting vigorously to sustain its power. On the other hand, Boff and others were aggressively working toward altering the Church into what they thought it should be.

Both have come out on the losing end of things. The liberation theologians viewed truth through widely held views of the people and human wisdom, leaving Scripture at the doorstep of the church. The Catholic Church was clinging to church tradition, as well as the power of the Pope to carry more authority than Scripture itself.

Liberation Theology Set Against the Bible

The Bible alone is,

2 Timothy 3:16 New Jerusalem Bible (NJB)

¹⁶ All scripture is inspired by God and useful for refuting error, for guiding people's lives and teaching them to be upright.

1 Corinthians 3:19 New Jerusalem Bible (NJB)

¹⁹ For the wisdom of the world is folly to God. As scripture says: He traps the crafty in the snare of their own cunning

Thus, how would we use God's Word to help us appreciate the concept of liberation theology?

You will not find the term liberation theology, but do we find the idea of working actively to combat social, political, and economic oppression? Well, it does touch on the idea of liberation, or the idea of being set free. Actually, this could well be seen as one of the themes running from Genesis to revelation.

Romans 8:12-21 New Jerusalem Bible (NJB)

¹² So then, my brothers, we have no obligation to human nature to be dominated by it. ¹³ If you do live in that way, you are doomed to die; but if by the Spirit you put to death the habits originating in the body, you will have life. ¹⁴ All who are guided by the Spirit of God are sons of God; ¹⁵ or what you

received was not the spirit of slavery to bring you back into fear; you received the Spirit of adoption, enabling us to cry out, 'Abba, Father!' [16] The Spirit himself joins with our spirit to bear witness that we are children of God. [17] And if we are children, then we are heirs, heirs of God and joint-heirs with Christ, provided that we share his suffering, so as to share his glory. [18] In my estimation, all that we suffer in the present time is nothing in comparison with the glory which is destined to be disclosed for us, [19] for the whole creation is waiting with eagerness for the children of God to be revealed. [20] It was not for its own purposes that creation had frustration imposed on it, but for the purposes of him who imposed it- [21] with the intention that the whole creation itself might be freed from its slavery to corruption and brought into the same glorious freedom as the children of God.

We can learn from Israelite history. They were liberated, or freed from slavery in Egypt about 3,525 years ago. How did this take place though, was it through a revolution, acts of violence, an uprising of the people? No, it was through divine intervention. In addition, how did it turn out when the Israelites chose to act independently of God? They were judged by him and suffered the consequences of their actions.

Keep in mind, we are talking about religious organizations involving themselves in social movements, and using violence to bring about change. However, Jesus Christ was not involved in the political issues or the social issues of his day. What happened when Peter tried to resort to violence to save the Son of God?

Matthew 26:51-52 New Jerusalem Bible (NJB)

51 And suddenly, one of the followers of Jesus grasped his sword and drew it; he struck the high priest's servant and cut off his ear. **52** Jesus then said, 'Put your sword back, for all who draw the sword will die by the sword.

This does not mean that Israel, which is more of a religious state, does not have the right to defend itself from Islamic terrorism. Moreover, we can certainly know that humankind is going to be liberated or freed from the greatest enemy of all, sin and death. However, this will not take place by some revolution, acts of violence, an uprising of the people.

True Liberation

Hebrews 6:1-2 New Jerusalem Bible (NJB)

¹ Let us leave behind us then all the elementary teaching about Christ and go on to its completion, without going over the fundamental doctrines again: the turning away from dead actions, faith in God, ² the teaching about baptisms and the laying, on of hands, about the resurrection of the dead and eternal judgment.

The resurrection is a foundational doctrine to our Christian faith. However, it does not compute with the world of humankind that is alienated from God. They see this as the only life there is, and so they are in pursuit of fleshly pleasures, to make the most of it. (1 Cor. 15:32) We on the other hand do not need to chase after the things that Satan's world has to offer.

Acts 17:32 English Standard Version (ESV)

³² Now when they heard of the resurrection of the dead, some mocked. But others said, "We will hear you again about this."

We need to look to at least two hopes that humans have the opportunity of having. Some are of new Israel and is seen as being given a kingdom, a chosen race, a royal priesthood, and ruling with Christ for a thousand years. There will be a need to investigate this, and this section will be a little more complex than any other part of this book. It is very important to all of us, so bear with me. I am going to quote some of the leading evangelical scholars at length.

Revelation 5:9-10 English Standard Version (ESV)

⁹ And they sang a new song, saying,

"Worthy are you to take the scroll
and to open its seals,
for you were slain, and by your blood you ransomed people for God
from every tribe and language and people and nation,
¹⁰ and you have made them a kingdom and priests to our God,
and they shall reign on[34] the earth."

Heavenly Hope

Revelation 14:1-4 English Standard Version (ESV)

---

[34] The Darby Bible DBY: they shall reign over the earth

¹ Then I looked, and behold, on Mount Zion stood the Lamb, and with him **144,000** who had his name and his Father's name written on their foreheads. ² And I heard a voice from heaven like the roar of many waters and like the sound of loud thunder. The voice I heard was like the sound of harpists playing on their harps, ³ and **they were singing a <u>new song</u>** before the throne and before the four living creatures and before the elders. **<u>No one could learn that song except</u> the 144,000 who had been redeemed from the earth**. ⁴ It is these who have not defiled themselves with women, for they are virgins. It is these who follow the Lamb wherever he goes. These have been redeemed from mankind as firstfruits for God and the Lamb

> The whole of chapter 14 is proleptic. As a summary of the Millennium (20:4–6), the first five verses feature the Lamb in place of the beast, the Lamb's followers with His and the Father's seal in place of the beast's followers with the mark of the beast, and the divinely controlled Mount Zion in place of the pagan-

controlled earth (Alford, Moffatt, Kiddle).[35]

Revelation 7:4 English Standard Version (ESV)

⁴ And I heard the number of the sealed, 144,000, sealed from every tribe of the sons of Israel

Various efforts have sought to determine the significance of the number 144,000. An understanding of the number as symbolical divides it into three of its multiplicands, 12 × 12 × 1000. From the symbolism of the three it is concluded that the number indicates fixedness and fullest completeness.[36] Twelve, a number of the tribes, is both squared and multiplied by a thousand. This is a twofold way of emphasizing completeness (Mounce). It thus affirms the full number of God's people to be brought through tribulation (Ladd). The symbolic approach points out the impossibility of taking the number literally. It is simply a vast number, less

---

[35] Robert L. Thomas, Revelation 8-22: An Exegetical Commentary (Chicago: Moody Publishers, 1995), 189.

[36] Alford, Greek Testament, 4:624; Charles, Revelation, 1:206; Lenski, Revelation, p. 154.

than a number indefinitely great (cf. 7:9), but greater than a large number designedly finite (e.g., 1,000, Rev. 20:2) (Lee). Other occurrences of the numerical components that are supposedly symbolic are also pointed out, 12 thousand in Rev. 21:16, 12 in Rev. 22:2, and 24, a multiple of 12, in Rev. 4:4. This is done to enhance the case for symbolism (Johnson). Though admittedly ingenious, the case for symbolism is exegetically weak. The principal reason for the view is a predisposition to make the 144,000 into a group representative of the church with which no possible numerical connection exists. No justification can be found for understanding the simple statement of fact in v. 4 as a figure of speech. It is a definite number in contrast with the indefinite number of 7:9. If it is taken symbolically, no number in the book can be taken literally. As God reserved 7,000 in the days of Ahab (1 Kings 19:18; Rom. 11:4), He will reserve 144,000 for Himself during the future Great Tribulation.[37] (Thomas,

---

[37] Bullinger, Apocalypse, p. 282. Geyser is correct in

Revelation 1-7: An Exegetical Commentary 1992, 473-74)

These ones are made up of those under the new covenant, the Law of Christ, those **called out of natural Israel**, the new Israelites, also known as the Israel of God. They are a chosen number that are to reign with Jesus as kings, priests, and judges. Therefore, we ask, what is the other hope?

The New Earth: The Earthly Hope

In the O[ld] T[estament] the kingdom of God is usually described in terms of a redeemed earth; this is especially clear in the book of Isaiah, where the final state of the universe is already called new heavens and a new

---

observing that the predominant concern of the Apocalypse is "the restoration [on earth] of the twelve tribes of Israel, their restoration as a twelve-tribe kingdom, in a renewed and purified city of David, under the rule of the victorious 'Lion of the Tribe of Judah, the Root of David' (5:5; 22:16)" (Albert Geyser, "The Twelve Tribes in Revelation: Judean and Judeo Christian Apocalypticism," NTS 23, no. 3 [July 1982]: 389). He is wrong, however, in his theory that this belief characterized the Judean church only and was not shared by Gentile Christianity spearheaded by Paul (ibid., p. 390).

earth (65:17; 66:22) The nature of this renewal was perceived only very dimly by OT authors, but they did express the belief that a humans ultimate destiny is an earthly one.[38] This vision is clarified in the N[ew] T[estament]. Jesus speaks of the "renewal" of the world (Matt 19:28), Peter of the restoration of all things (Acts 3:21). Paul writes that the universe will be redeemed by God from its current state of bondage (Rom. 8:18-21). This is confirmed by Peter, who describes the new heavens and the new earth as the Christian's hope (2 Pet. 3:13). Finally, the book of Revelation includes a glorious vision of the end of the present universe and the creation of a new universe, full of righteousness and the presence of God. The vision is confirmed by God in the awesome declaration: "I am making everything new!" (Rev. 21:1-8).

The new heavens and the new earth will be the renewed creation that

---

[38] It is unwise to speak of the written Word of God as if it were of human origin, saying 'OT authors express the belief,' when what was written is the meaning and message of what God wanted to convey by means of the human author.

will fulfill the purpose for which God created the universe. It will be characterized by the complete rule of God and by the full realization of the final goal of redemption: "Now the dwelling of God is with men" (Rev. 21:3).

The fact that the universe will be created anew[39] shows that God's goals for humans is not an ethereal and disembodied existence, but a bodily existence on a perfected earth. The scene of the beatific vision is the new earth. The spiritual does not exclude the created order and will be fully realized only within a perfected creation. (Elwell 2001, 828-29)

What does the Bible make quite clear about God's original intentions? God created the earth to be inhabited, to be filled with perfect humans, who are over the animals, and under the sovereignty of God. (Gen 1:28; 2:8, 15; Ps 104:5; 115:16; Eccl 1:4) Sin did not dissuade God from his plans (Isa. 45:18); hence, he has liberated or saved redeemable humankind by

---

[39] Create anew does not mean a complete destruction followed by a re-creation, but instead a renewal of the present universe.

Jesus ransom sacrifice. It seems that the Bible offers two hopes to redeemed humans, **(1) a heavenly hope**, or **(2) an earthly hope**. It also seems that those with the heavenly hope are limited in number, and are going to heaven to rule with Christ as kings, priests, and judges either **on** the earth or **over** the earth from heaven. It seems that those with the earthly hope are going to receive eternal life here on a paradise earth as originally intended.

What about Now?

Certainly, any rational person would desire to help those impoverished and oppressed persons around the world, who are just barely surviving life. Jesus had great empathy for the poor of his day. Note how Jesus was moved,

Matthew 9:36 English Standard Version (ESV)

³⁶ When he saw the crowds, he had compassion for them, because they were harassed and helpless, like sheep without a shepherd.

Moreover, Jesus offered these ones, and all others who heard him, liberation or freedom, if they would just respond to his message.

John 8:32 English Standard Version (ESV)

³² and you will know the truth, and the truth will set you free."

The question that begs to be asked is, 'are Christian ministers today following the Bible by offering liberation theology for the poor and oppressed?'

An Erroneous Philosophy

The short answer would be, no. First, we would have to note once more that Jesus did not advocate uprisings and violence, or involving oneself in the political arena of his day. In addition, the minister or pastor has the primary responsibility to care for the same thing Jesus cared for, the spirituality of the person. It may surprise most when I inform the reader that the countries that are not oppressed and are financially well off, are struggling the most spiritually. The United States used to be the leader in sending out missionaries to other countries, now they are at the top of the list for receiving missionaries. There are 350,000 churches in the United States, and 80 percent are stagnant, with 19 percent gaining members only by transfer from one church to another or they are growing through childbirth and less than 1 percent by actual conversion. The United Kingdom has a church attendance rate of ten percent. The United States and Europe, notwithstanding their current economic situation, have enjoyed a high level of living for decades, yet they suffer from extreme spiritual apathy. Dishonesty, immorality, child abuse and abuse of the elderly, violent crime as well as greed, to name just a few problems that are rampant. The sad story is in many places interest in God is all but dead.

2 Timothy 3:1-5 English Standard Version (ESV)

¹ But understand this that in the last days there will come times of difficulty. ² For people will be lovers of self, lovers of money, proud, arrogant, abusive, disobedient to their parents, ungrateful, unholy, ³ heartless, unappeasable, slanderous, without self-control, brutal, not loving good, ⁴ treacherous, reckless, swollen with conceit, lovers of pleasure rather than lovers of God, ⁵ having the appearance of godliness, but denying its power. Avoid such people.

If we look at what Jesus did in his three and half year ministry, we will discover that he was not using liberation theology to help the poor and oppressed. Moreover, we must consider the fact that he is our example, which we are obligated to pattern ourselves after. (1 Peter 2:21) Jesus lived under the Roman Empire, but locally under a colonial power, which was quite oppressive to its people, especially the poor. Jesus' family was poor and oppressed, but he was not moved to affiliate himself with the Jewish group known as the Zealots, a Jewish party opposed to the Romans. They were militant nationalists who did much to provoke the Jewish revolt against the Romans in 66 C.E. The helpless during Jesus' ministry years was victimized by the Jewish religious leaders, the greedy tax collectors, and the wealthy class. (Matthew 22:21; Luke 3:12, 13; 20:46, 47) Even so, Jesus never involved himself in any uprising, and revolt, or even in the politics of the day, trying to improve the lot of his fellow Jews, not to mention his own family. Jesus chose to,

Matthew 4:23 English Standard Version (ESV)

[23] And he went throughout all Galilee, teaching in their synagogues and proclaiming the gospel of the kingdom and healing every disease and every affliction among the people.

Lastly, a minister of religion who seeks to solve his problems through political means, aside from voting, is not going about it God's way. It may be called a theology, but that does not make it biblical. What did Jesus say of himself and his disciples?

John 17:16 English Standard Version (ESV)

¹⁶ They are not of the world, just as I am not of the world.

Jesus' half-brother and pillar in the Christian Church in Jerusalem also wrote on this issue,

James 4:4 English Standard Version (ESV)

⁴ You adulterous people! Do you not know that friendship with the world is enmity with God? Therefore whoever wishes to be a friend of the world makes himself an enemy of God.

How Can We Really Help the Poor?

The poor lands of the Third World have a greater spirituality than the wealthy counties. If one were to live by the Bible principles, applying them in a balanced mature way, they would fare better in these difficult times. Thus, we help the poor by not being sidetracked from the commission that we were given. If Satan and his world of fallen humankind can get us busy trying to rescue a fallen situation, he will have been more effective at his commission.

Matthew 28:19-20 English Standard Version (ESV)

[19] Go therefore and make disciples of all nations ... [20] teaching them to observe all that I have commanded you. And behold, I am with you always, to the end of the age."

A time is coming when we will see divine intervention into the oppressed world that we are living in, but that day has yet to arrive. We need to look to the King, Jesus Christ, as the one who will bring about change.

Revelation 11:15, 18 English Standard Version (ESV)

[15] Then the seventh angel blew his trumpet, and there were loud voices in heaven, saying, "The kingdom of the world has become the kingdom of our Lord and of his Christ, and he shall reign forever and ever."

[18] The nations raged,
   but your wrath came,
   and the time for the dead to be judged,
and for rewarding your servants, the prophets and saints,
   and those who fear your name,
   both small and great,
and for destroying the destroyers of the earth."

Revelation 21:3-4 English Standard Version (ESV)

³ And I heard a loud voice from the throne saying, "Behold, the dwelling place of God is with man. He will dwell with them, and they will be his people, and God himself will be with them as their God. ⁴ He will wipe away every tear from their eyes, and death shall be no more, neither shall there be mourning, nor crying, nor pain anymore, for the former things have passed away."

We return to the question of, are we really helping the poor now? Keep in mind and have faith in what Jesus said,

John 8:32 English Standard Version (ESV)

³² and you will know the truth, and the truth will set you free."

The truth of the Scripture will remove many of the obstacles that the poor face, by applying God's Word more fully in their lives. Moreover, there are so many qualities that we must possess when we take off the old person of the world and put on the new person (Col 3:9-10) There are poor persons abusing and drugs to cope with their problems, leaving their children hungry. You have others wasting money on gambling, believing they can just win enough. However, if they put God's Kingdom first and live according to His righteous standards, in one way or another, the physical necessities of life are provided, by their living either by Christian principles, or by the Christian congregation offsetting their needs.

If you have a ship that is sinking, and you are trying to help those on that ship, who are open to the help, while others are standing around having a good time, refusing the help; then, it is no fault other than their own when the ship goes down and they are not on a lifeboat. We are to help our Christian brothers and sisters, and to do what we can for our neighbors, but we best help the world of humankind by warning them that the ship is going down.

1 Timothy 4:8 English Standard Version (ESV)

⁸ for while bodily training is of some value, godliness is of value in every way, as it holds promise for the present life and also for the life to come.

BASIC TEACHING: Does It Matter Which Bible Translation?

Leland Ryken

Wheaton College

The Bible Translation Debate

UNTIL THE MIDDLE OF THE TWENTIETH CENTURY, all major English Bible translations were based on the premise that the goal of Bible translation is to take the reader as close as possible to the words that the biblical authors actually wrote. William Tyndale, the fountainhead of English Bible translation, even made up English words like *intercession*, *atonement*, *scapegoat*, *and Passover* in order to do justice to the very words of the biblical text.

Equally striking are the italicized words in the King James Version. Surely many English readers are mystified by the italicizing of words and phrases in the KJV. Following the lead of the Geneva Bible (1560), the King James translators were so scrupulous about keeping the record clear as to what the biblical authors actually wrote that they italicized words that the translators added for the sake of clarity or fluency in English. By contrast, modern dynamic equivalent translators hope to keep readers in the dark regarding changes that have been made to the original. If that seems like a doubtful statement, I will just adduce the example of a colleague of mine who was given permission to produce an interlinear version of the NIV New Testament. A high-ranking person in the publishing house expressed surprise that this permission had been granted since it would show at once how many words in the NIV have no corresponding word in the Greek original.

Exactly what happened in the middle of the twentieth century?

All major translations before the rise of dynamic equivalent translations were based on the principle of essentially literal translation, also known as verbal equivalence. This translation philosophy strives to give an equivalent English word or phrase for all words found in the original text of the Bible. The goal is to convey everything that it is in the original-- but not more than is in the original or less than is there.

The new translation philosophy is called dynamic equivalence, but that designation is very inadequate to cover all that modernizing translations actually do. In fact, equivalence is not usually, what these translations give. Usually they give a substitution or replacement for what the original says. Additionally, dynamic equivalent translators omit material from material in the original and add to it. Dynamic equivalent translators feel no compulsion to reproduce in English the words that the biblical authors wrote. In fact, the prefaces to these translations, as well as surrounding published materials and interviews, hold verbal equivalence up to scorn. These prefaces and translators are bold to claim that a translation that departs from the words of the biblical authors is often more accurate than translations that reproduce the words of the original text.

Are my claims really true? I will give an example of each of the three common maneuvers of dynamic equivalent translators.

Omitting material from the Bible. The most plentiful parts of the Bible where this is done are passages with figurative language. In 1 Corinthians 16:9, Paul speaks metaphorically of "a wide door" that has "opened" to him (ESV). Dynamic equivalent translators who believe that modern readers cannot understand metaphors simply remove the wide door from sight: "a good opportunity" (New Century

Version); "a wonderful opportunity" (Contemporary English Version); "a real opportunity" (Good News Bible). As all of this license unfolds before us, we need to ask, who gave us the metaphor of the wide door in the first place? The answer should be the writers of the Bible writing under the inspiration of the Holy Spirit.

Offering a substitute for what is in the Bible. Omission of material from the original text is often accompanied by a substitution for what a biblical author wrote. In Psalm 73, the poet recalls his crisis of faith in metaphoric terms: "my steps had nearly slipped" (v. 2b, ESV). Several dynamic equivalent translations give us a substitute for the image of slipping steps: "I had almost lost my faith" (New Century Version); "my faith was almost gone" (Good News Bible). As one expert on Bible translation exclaims, "This is not translation at all but merely replacement."

Adding commentary to what the biblical authors wrote. Dynamic equivalent translators incessantly add commentary to what the original text gives us. Of course, the reader has no clue as to where the original text of the Bible ends and the commentary of the translators begin. In Psalm 23:5a, David writes, "You anoint my head with oil." There is no dispute that this is what the original text says. Nevertheless, dynamic equivalent translators feel an overpowering urge to add commentary beyond the biblical text: "You welcome me as a guest, anointing my head with oil" (NLT). Unless you can read the Hebrew original or have the good fortune to be familiar with an essentially literal translation, you cannot answer the question of where the original text ends and the translator's commentary begins. Of course, you *should* be able to trust your English Bible not to mislead you.

Why would translators do these things?

Why do translators feel free to engage in the kind of license I have noted? There are several answers. First, Bible translation took a wrong turn when the concept of a target audience became enthroned. This concept envisions an audience of limited linguistic and theological abilities. The almost universally accepted criterion of dynamic equivalent translations is a reader with the linguistic and theological comprehension of a sixth-grader. With this target audience firmly ensconced, the entire translation is then slanted toward the assumed abilities of this audience. I agree with the verdict of Dr. John McArthur, who in an endorsement of one of my books spoke of translators who are more concerned with the human audience than the divine author of the Bible is.

Additionally, the entire dynamic equivalent enterprise is based on the premise that the Bible is an inadequate book that needs correction. All we need to do is read the prefaces of these translations and observe what the translators have done to see that the translators believe that they can communicate better than the biblical authors did. The biblical authors used metaphors, but modern readers cannot understand metaphoric language. The biblical authors used theological language, but theological language is beyond modern readers. Etc., etc. The view of biblical authors that emerges from this branch of Bible translation is that they are inept and in need of correction. It is no wonder that half a century of dynamic equivalent translations has made the following formula omnipresent in evangelical circles: "now what the biblical author was *trying to say* is . . . ."

What is at stake in the current debate?

Two things chiefly are at stake in the current debate between the rival translation philosophies. One is whether we can trust our English Bibles. I propose that we cannot trust dynamic equivalent translations to put us in contact with the Bible that God inspired the human authors to write. What is the assumption (completely legitimate) that we all make when we hold a book in our hands? Surely that the publisher has put into print the words that the author wrote. Dynamic equivalent translations consistently betray that trust.

Additionally, English readers need to choose between the actual Bible that God inspired his authors to write, or a substitute for that Bible. I resonate completely with an emailer who wrote to me that he was raised on an essentially literal Bible, gravitated to a dynamic equivalent translation through peer pressure, and returned to an essentially literal translation after reading one of my books. His parting shot was that "it was as though someone had given me my Bible back."

When dynamic equivalence swept the field half a century ago, people were so intoxicated by the exciting new view of Bible translation that they did not pay attention to what was actually happening. The time has come for sober reality. I would urge readers of the English Bible to practice what an advertising slogan of several years ago advocated: *Accept no substitute.*

BASIC TEACHING: Was Job a Real Historical Person?

Moses was the author of the book of Job. It was written in a place called the wilderness. The writing was completed by Moses about c.[40] 1473 B.C.E. The time the book covered was over 140 years between 1657 B.C.E. and 1473 B.C.E.

Before defending Job as a real historical person, we might take a couple paragraphs, to answer why we have said that Moses is the author of Job and have established an about date as the time of writing, especially when source books have this to say, "no one knows when or by whom Job was written."[41] The oldest tradition among the Jewish and early Christians scholars has Moses as the author.

Job lived in Uz, "the evidence supports the conclusion that Job's land of Uz was E of Edom

---

[40] c. is an abbreviation for circa (used before dates) to indicate that it is approximate or estimated

[41] David S. Dockery, Trent C. Butler, Christopher L. Church et al., Holman Bible Handbook (Nashville, TN: Holman Bible Publishers, 1992), 312.

in the Arabian Desert."[42] Job's trial can be inferred to have come sometime after Abraham's day, because it was a time when "there [was] none like him on the earth, a blameless and upright man, who fears God and turns away from evil." (1:8) This time period would fit logically between the death of Joseph (1657 B.C.E.), a man like Job, and the time of Moses, who is like Job as well, "blameless and upright man, who fears God and turns away from evil." Job surpassed all others in pure worship at a time, when Israel was polluted by the demon worship of Egypt. Moreover, the context of Job chapter one is indicative of patriarchal times, as opposed to the period after the Exodus from Egypt, in which there was the Mosaic Law. (Amos 3:2; Eph. 2:12) "For not only does he not mention the Law or the exodus, but he is pictured as a wealthy nomad (Job 1:3; 42:12) who is still offering sacrifices himself (Job 1:5; 42:8)."[43] Therefore, when we consider the long life of Job, the book covers a time between 1657 B.C.E. and 1473 B.C.E., the

---

[42] Geoffrey W. Bromiley, vol. 4, The International Standard Bible Encyclopedia, Revised (Wm. B. Eerdmans, 1988; 2002), 959.

[43] Chad Brand, Charles Draper, Archie England et al., *Holman Illustrated Bible Dictionary* (Nashville, TN: Holman Bible Publishers, 2003), 924.

year they entered the Promised Land, and the death of Moses. Thus, Moses penned the book of Job after the death of Job, but just before they entered the Promised Land, of which Moses was not privileged. Job 1:8; 42:16, 17.

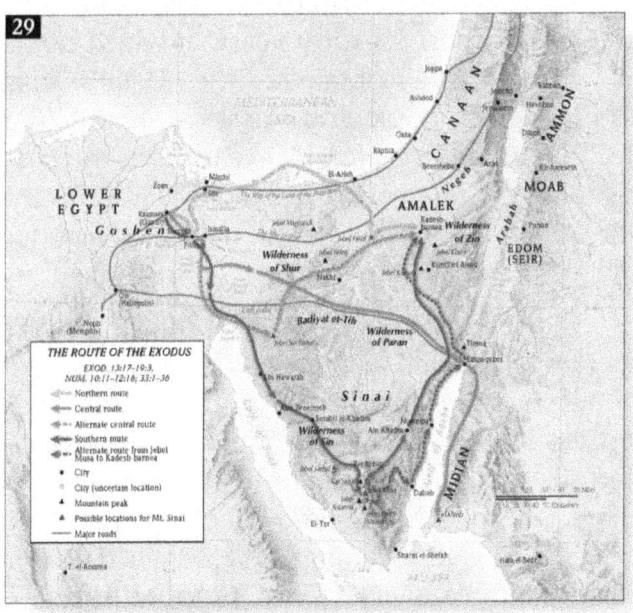

The book of Job uses a dynamic genuine style of Hebrew poetry, which makes it apparent that it was originally composed in the language of Moses, Hebrew. In addition, the parts that is in what is in prose, language that is not poetry, bear stronger similarity to the Pentateuch than the rest of the Bible. Once Moses turned forty, he would spend the next forty years of his life in Midian, which was located not too far from Uz, the homeland of Job. While there for four decades, Moses could have gained the details that went into the writing of Job. Moses would later pass by Job's homeland while the Israelites were wondering in the wilderness for forty years, at which point, he could have obtained the details that concluded the book. Job's trial was about 1613 B.C.E., and he lived for 140-years after the trial, meaning his death was about 1473 B.C.E., the very year the Israelites entered the Promised Land.

The supernatural forces that afflict Job and his family, as well as the poetic form in 39 out of 42 chapters of Job give some scholars their justification to question Job as a real historical person. Job is thought to be a fictional character, which is used like an extended parable, to give meaning to those who were in Babylonian captivity. They propose that the book was composed sometime after 537 B.C.E., after their return from exile in Babylon. The reason offered for such a late date of composition is that there are frequent loan words from Aramaic, as well as pure monotheism in the mindset of the five persons, involved in the interchange, within the story of Job.

It should be observed that the person who makes such propositions is under the weight of defending his or her position, and the Christian needs to leave that weight to them, making them do the work that they thought was going to be on us, by their offering up an accusation such as this. However, for now, we will offer an answer to such a skeptical theory of a fictional person, written almost a thousand years after its actual date of being written. Thus, there is ample evidence to establish Job as a real historical person, as well the details of his life.

We begin with the fact that if we look to verse one of the book of Job, it clearly states that Job actually existed. There are no literary suggestions as to other than, we are dealing with real history.

Job 1:1 English Standard Version (ESV)

¹<u>There was a man</u> in the land of Uz whose name was Job, and that man was blameless and upright, one who feared God and turned away from evil.

As was stated, the author, Moses, wrote in such a matter of fact way, being no different from other places within Scripture that is taken as being historically true.

1 Samuel 1:1 English Standard Version (ESV)

¹<u>There was a certain</u> man of Ramathaim-zophim of the hill country of Ephraim whose name was Elkanah the son of Jeroham, son of Elihu, son of Tohu, son of Zuph, an Ephrathite.

Luke 1:5 English Standard Version (ESV)

⁵In the days of Herod, king of Judea, <u>there was a priest named Zechariah</u>, of the division of Abijah. And he had a wife from the daughters of Aaron, and her name was Elizabeth.

If we are taking the other statements within Scripture, such as those found in 1 Samuel and Luke, as well as elsewhere, as being historical, it only seems reasonable that we give Job the same consideration.

Other portions of Scripture rise up, as a witness to Job being a real historical person. Ezekiel 14:14, 20, Job is named by God along with Daniel and Noah as examples of righteous ones. In the book of James (5:11), there is a reference to job as an example of patience in the midst of difficult times. If Job were not a real historical person, it would invalidate God or James using him as such, making these verses meaningless.

Ezekiel 14:14, 20 English Standard Version (ESV)

[14]even if these three men, Noah, Daniel, and Job, were in it [Israel], they would deliver but their own lives by their righteousness, declares the Lord GOD. [20]even if Noah, Daniel, and Job were in it, as I live, declares the Lord GOD, they would deliver neither son nor daughter. They would deliver but their own lives by their righteousness.

James 5:11 English Standard Version (ESV)

[11]Behold, we consider those blessed who remained steadfast. You have heard of the steadfastness of Job, and you have seen the purpose of the Lord, how the Lord is compassionate and merciful.

In Ezekiel, the reader discovers God confirming Job as being just as historical as either Noah or Daniel. If one argued that Job was only a mythological character, this would throw a shadow of doubt on Noah and Daniel as well. Worse still, it could be suggested that even God was deceived as to Job's historicity, by his use of him as a real historical character, while the modern-day critic got it right!

To discount Job because of the debate between Jehovah and Satan the Devil at the outset of the book is no reason for discounting the book as historical. If this were the case, how are we to handle the gospels of Matthew and Luke, with their giving us the temptation and conversation between Jesus Christ and Satan the Devil? As to the linguistic argument, Bible scholar Gleason L. Archer penned the following:

The linguistic argument based on the presence of terms more characteristic of Aramaic than Hebrew is tenuous indeed. The Aramaic language was evidently known and used in North Arabia for a long period of time. The numerous first-millennium inscriptions of the North Arabian Nabateans are almost invariably written in Aramaic, and commercial relations with Aramaic-speaking peoples probably began before 2000 B.C. Jacob's father-in-law, Laban, was certainly Aramaic speaking (cf. Gen. 31:47). Commercial contacts with the great Syrian center of Ebla were very extensive as early as 2400 B.C. (though the Eblaites themselves seem to have spoken an Amorite dialect, rather than Aramaic).

Furthermore, it should be pointed out that the extent of Aramaic influence has been somewhat overrated. A. Guillaume ("The Unity of the Book of Job," Annual of Leeds University, Oriental Sec. 14 [1962–63]: 26–27) has convincingly argued that there are no demonstrable Aramaisms in the speeches of Elihu (Job 32–37), which reputedly have the highest incidence of them. He contends that nearly all of them are terms existing in Arabic that happen to have cognates in Aramaic as well. He deals with no less than twenty-five examples of this, citing the Arabic originals in every case. Since the setting of the narrative is in Uz, located somewhere in North Arabia, this admixture of Arabic and Aramaic vocabulary is exactly what should be expected in the text of Job, whether it was originally composed in Hebrew (which is rather unlikely), or whether it was translated out of an earlier text written in the language prevalent in North Arabia during the pre-Mosaic period.[44]

Having considered the above evidence, there is no alternative, but to accept the book of Job as a historical work, with real historical persons, and historical events between 1657 B.C.E. and 1473 B.C.E. Thus, Jehovah God used this historical hero, in the same way He

---

[44] Gleason L. Archer, New International Encyclopedia of Bible Difficulties, Zondervan's Understand the Bible Reference Series (Grand Rapids, MI: Zondervan Publishing House, 1982), 236.

used Noah and Daniel. The same holds true for James use of Job as an example of how we should react when under difficult times. From James, we learn that Jehovah God was 'compassionate and merciful to Job,' extending his life, restoring his health, and giving him more children. This is hardly possible if Job were a fictional character.

Other Books Authored by Edward D. Andrews

BASIC TEACHINGS OF THE BIBLE Questions Christians Ask—Biblical Answers[45]

45

http://www.christianpublishers.org/apps/webstore/products/show/4676307

Basic Teachings of the Bible is going to be a series of books that covers the Bible's position on the life questions that Christians and non-Christians ask themselves and others,

- Is it a Sin to Drink Alcoholic Beverages?
- Is it Wrong for Christians to Flirt?
- Are Women Allowed to Teach the Church?
- Should infants be baptized?
- Is hell a place of eternal torment?
- Do We Possess a Soul or Are We a Soul?
- Is Gambling a Sin?
- Why Does an All-Loving God Permit Pain, Suffering and Wickedness to Continue?
- Who Is the Avenging Messenger that Destroys the Wicked Ones?
- Does God Step in and Solve Our Every Problem, Because We are Faithful?
- If Homosexuals Are Born Genetically Predisposed, Is That Not of God?
- Is Anger Always Wrong?
- What About the Rod of Discipline of Proverbs 22:15?
- Has Fate Already Written Your Future?
- Who Is the Antichrist?

These are the type of basic Bible questions that are discussed and debated, before and after church services, at Christian gatherings, and on the internet. There are literally hundreds of them. These are questions that Bible critics might raise as well, which Christians have struggled to answer and now will have a simplified biblical response. The answers to these Bible questions are given from the Bible itself, as well as reasoning from the Scriptures. If the texts are straightforward, which answer the life question, the text alone will be used. However, if the text is difficult to understand, reasoning from the Scriptures will be used with the text. Some of the topics will be answered in just 2-3 pages, while some may take up to 15 pages or more. It is hoped that the reader will find the answers as additional evidence demonstrating that the Bible is the best source for guiding one's life. This publication is volume 1 of numerous volumes to come.

WALK HUMBLY WITH YOUR GOD: Putting God's Purpose First in Your Life [46]

The purpose of this book is to serve as a guide to all Christians, who are interested in walking with God, living a good and productive Christian life, carrying ourselves rightly in the love of God. What does this involve? We must visit the words of Jesus Christ, as he similarly says, "If you keep my commandments, you will abide in my love, just as I have kept my Father's commandments and abide in his love." (John 15:10) To evidence the love of God in our lives, we need to apply the Word of God in everyday life. Jesus also said, "If you know these things, happy you are if you do them."—John 13:17.

---

[46] http://www.christianpublishers.org/apps/webstore/products/show/4676342

It is my genuine expectation that this publication will help you to more fully evidence the love of God in your life and thus can fulfill the wishes of the Creator himself, "Be wise, my son, and make my heart glad, that I may answer him who reproaches me."—Proverbs 27:11.

APPLYING GOD'S WORD MORE FULLY IN YOUR LIFE: How to Broaden and Deepen Your Understanding of God's Word[47]

Hundreds of millions of Christians around the world are lacking the basic knowledge of the Bible's teachings. Moreover, they are therefore, unable to take advantage of the full happiness of partaking in joint worship of God; they need to have their powers of discernment trained by constant practice to distinguish good from evil, they need to leave the elementary doctrine of Christ and move on to maturity. This book has been penned for that very purpose, to help all Christians to increase and expand their understanding of God's Word and to apply it

---

[47] http://www.christianpublishers.org/apps/webstore/products/show/4676315

more fully in their lives. Be aware that this book will ask questions that are designed, to help us investigate our inner-self.

MISREPRESENTING JESUS: Debunking Bart D. Ehrman's Misquoting Jesus[48]

Edward Andrews boldly answers the challenges Bart D. Ehrman puts against the divine inspiration and authority of the Bible. By glimpsing into the life of Bart D. Ehrman and following along his course of academic studies, Andrews helps the reader to understand the biases, assumptions, and shortcomings supporting Ehrman's arguments. Using sound logic, technical exegesis, and conservative interpretation, Andrews helps scholars overcome the teachings of biblical errancy that Ehrman propagates.

---

[48] http://www.christianpublishers.org/apps/webstore/products/show/4672868

"A sometimes complex area has been made very palatable and enjoyable to read. Dare I say-- even quite exciting!" —Online reviewer

THE TEXT OF THE NEW TESTAMENT: A Beginner's Guide to New Testament Textual Criticism[49]

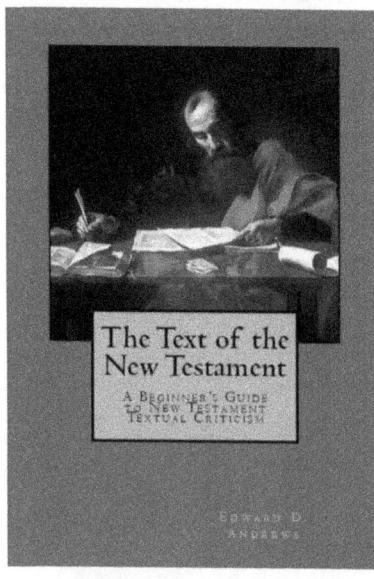

Many critics of the Bible say that we cannot know what was said, because we do not have the originals. This is a false claim, because we can get back to the originals by restoring what was there through the science of textual criticism, and a restored text, is the same as the originals, minus being on the same original papyrus.

Starting with the basics, Edward D. Andrews guides you through New Testament textual criticism. Starting with the threat to the authority and authenticity of the New

---

[49] http://www.christianpublishers.org/apps/webstore/products/show/4676238

Testament text (Bible critics), The Text of the New Testament leads you through each aspect of textual studies to prepare you for studying the Bible as a student of the textual history. Even more importantly, Andrews presents arguments to defend the Bible's authority and accuracy against the latest onslaught of atheist and agnostic scholarship undermining the Bible as divinely inspired, inerrant and irrefutable. Andrews gives the student the history of the text, explaining the art and science of textual criticism, offering the reader a word picture of the ancient books, as well as the basics of paleography (dating manuscripts). In addition, he explains how we can restore what the original text said, the different methods of textual criticism, taking the reader through the process of publishing the original New Testament books, along with the 1,400-year period of corruption by copyists, culminating with the 400 years of restoration, and so much more. This will enable the Bible student to defend himself against those who wish to cast doubt on the trustworthiness of our Greek New Testament text.

THE COMPLETE GUIDE TO BIBLE TRANSLATION: Bible Translation Choices and Translation Principles[50]

It is a daunting task for the new Bible student to walk into a store for the purpose of purchasing a Bible. Immediately, he is met with shelves upon shelves of more than 100 different English translation choices: AMP, AT, ASV, BLE, CEB, CEV, ERV, ESV, HCSB, IB, ISV, JB, KJ21, LB, MLB, NAB, NASB, NCV, NEB, NET, NJB, NIV, NIVI, NIRV, NKJV, NLT, NLV, NRSV, REB, RSV, RVB, SEB, TEV, TNIV, WE and on and on. He is even further bewildered when he realizes that, in addition to the standard format, there are different formats within each translation: a reference Bible, a study Bible, a life application Bible, an

---

[50] http://www.christianpublishers.org/apps/webstore/products/show/4676262

archaeology Bible. He further notices that some translations claim to be Essentially Literal, while others claim to be Dynamic Equivalent (thought for thought), which only serves to increase his confusion.

The goal of THE COMPLETE GUIDE TO BIBLE TRANSLATION is to offer those new to the subject an overview of the history and methods, aims and results of the Bible translation process.

In addition, the reader will gain an appreciation of the work and lifetime efforts of hundreds of Bible scholars over the past 450-years, who have labored, so that we can say that we have many very good translations that are a mirror like reflection of the original, in translation. The reader will also find that he or she has a renewed confidence in the reliability of the Bible. Finally, the reader will be able to determine for himself or herself, which translations are the best for study and research.

YOUR GUIDE FOR DEFENDING THE BIBLE: Self-Education of the Bible Made Easy[51]

LET ME ASK YOU SOME QUESTIONS:

(1) Do you want to waste your hard-earned money by buying the wrong books?

(2) Do have some basic Bible knowledge, and would love to have more?

(3) Do you wish that you could be better at sharing your faith, defending what you know to be true?

(4) Do you fear those tough Bible questions?

(5) Do you want to be able to defend God's Word as true, inerrant and inspired?

---

[51] http://www.christianpublishers.org/apps/webstore/products/show/4676266

(6) Are you tired of the Bible scholars having all the knowledge?

(7) Do you want to have confidence when you are talking to others about the Bible?

(8) Do you want to learn how to study better, and more efficiently?

(9) Do you want to accomplish these things in the most productive way possible?

If one were to go on any discussion board on the worldwide internet, he or she would find hundreds of millions in ongoing, unending debates on countless websites about God's Word and its reliability and inspiration. In other words, 'is the Bible the Word of God?' Sadly, the reader of this book will find many people today, who are losing faith in the belief that the Bible is the inspired, inerrant Word of God. Why?

Liberal-progressive Christianity has overtaken conservative Christianity in the last 70-years. These are the ones, who claim that the Bible is a book by man alone, not inspired; being subject to errors, contradictions, and "unscientific." Other critics argue that the Bible is nothing more than a collection of myths and legends. Still, others argue that archaeology and

Biblical chronology cannot be harmonized. Other critics claim that the Gospels of Mathew, Mark, Luke and John are not historically accurate. Others still, argue that Jesus was not divine, claiming he was merely a traveling sage.

Your Guide for Defending the Bible offers the Bible student an introduction to many different subject areas that will help him or her to follow the following biblical counsel:

BE PREPARED TO MAKE A DEFENSE

1 Peter 3:15 English Standard Version (ESV)

But in your hearts honor Christ the Lord as holy, always being prepared to make a defense to anyone who asks you for a reason for the hope that is in you

CONTEND FOR THE FAITH

Jude 1:3 English Standard Version (ESV)

Beloved, although I was very eager to write to you about our common salvation, I found it necessary to write appealing to you to contend for the faith that was once for all delivered to the saints.

HELP THOSE WHO DOUBT

Jude 1:22-23 English Standard Version (ESV)

And have mercy on those who doubt; save others by snatching them out of the fire;

AN INTRODUCTION TO BIBLE DIFFICULTIES: So-called Errors and Contradictions[52]

The Bible is loaded with thousands of difficult, challenging passages-many of which become obstacles in the development of our faith. These difficulties arise out of differences in culture, language, needs, religious and political organization, not to mention between 2,000 and 3,500 years of separation. Calling attention to these difficulties and sifting out the misconceptions, Edward Andrews defends the inerrancy of the Bible, clarifies apparent contradictions, and arms you with what you need to defend your faith in the Bible.

---

[52] http://www.christianpublishers.org/apps/webstore/products/show/4676280

www.ingramcontent.com/pod-product-compliance
Lightning Source LLC
Chambersburg PA
CBHW051754040426
42446CB00007B/368